A Third Party Evaluation Report on the Informatization of Chinese Courts

Editor in Chief: Tian He

Executive Editor: Lv Yanbin

Paths International Ltd

中国社会科学出版社
CHINA SOCIAL SCIENCES PRESS

Abstract

The court informatization as an important component of the national informatization is essential for the people's courts to uphold social fairness and justice, and to meet the demands of the public for justice. It marks the transformation of trial and management, being itself a system engineering powering the modernization of the trial system and capabilities. The Institute of Law of CASS has carried out a third party evaluation of the court information development in China with regard to its implementation of justice for the people, promotion of judicial openness, regulation of exercising judicial power, upgrading of judicial capability and its service for the state governance. In general the infrastructure of the court information interconnection has been upgraded to version 2.0, having completed the construction of an information network integrating five major network services, applied in ten domains such as judicial services, trial enforcement and judicial administration, and concentrated the management of three databases in terms of trial and enforcement, judicial human resources, and judicial administration. Yet problems still exist in the informatization process such as those of outdated ideas and thinking, unbalanced development, failure of implementation of planning, inefficient application, an underdeveloped management mechanism and unqualified personnel. Future painstaking efforts are expected to be devoted to a better service for the public, trial and enforcement, and judicial administration on the way to upgrading the court information to version 3.0.

Key words: court informatization; justice for the people; judicial transparency; trial system; trial capability

Foreword

Since the 1990s, global science and technology has been progressing every single day, with internet and big data having become an important orientation of the times and the most significant characteristics of the global economic society as well. Therefore promoting information development is becoming not only a top concern of the state, but a demanded work for the court. The informatization of courts is defined as an endeavor and process in which the courts take initiatives to upgrade judicial credibility and to uphold legal justice by developing and implementing various types of information systems utilizing information technology in their collection, processing, storage, sharing and exploration of all kinds of information emerging from trials for promoting judicial transparency and justice for the people to the public, and for standardizing the exercise of internal judicial power and improving both the quality and efficiency of court performance. Being an important component of the state informatization, the court informatization is undergoing a profound self-revolution within the judicial system, which is not only transforming the trial mode, but improving judicial capability and optimizing the judicial structure for the construction of an innovative trial mode. And at the same time it serves as an important means to provide better services for the public and to realize the fundamental goal of justice for the people. Therefore, the development of the court information is a key solution for the court to tackle a series of deep-level issues such as how to better achieve social fairness and justice and how to meet the judicial needs of the public in the New Era, being itself an important part of the judicial reform.

Recent years have witnessed remarkable achievements in judicial transparency, justice for the people, and the betterment of trial quality and efficiency as well as the standardization of judicial administration, as a result of the great initiatives by the Chinese courts in their construction of the court information network under the guidance of the overall strategy for ruling the country by law, and in accordance with the idea of "Big data, large scale, great service" while striving to provide good services for the people, trial, and judicial administration.

General Secretary Xi Jinping has pointed out that "there would be no modernization without informatization". In order to have a working knowledge of the status quo of the informatization of the Chinese courts, the Institute of Law of CASS has conducted a third party evaluation of the informatization of courts focusing on its role in the standardization of judicial power, improvement of judicial capabilities and practices in achieving justice for the people, for assessing its achievements, analyzing its existing difficulties and exploring its future development.

The informatization of courts started as early as May of 1996 when the Supreme People's Court organized the "Conference on the Communication and Computer Application in the National Courts" in Jiangsu, on which decision was made, in an arrangement of the computer network construction in the state courts, that all together eight high courts and those under their jurisdictions respectively in Beijing, Shanghai, Jiangsu, Liaoning, Henan, Hainan, Guangdong, and Fujian provinces were designated as experimental units for the court computer network construction, and thereby having formulated *Plan for the Construction of the Computer Information Network for the National Courts* and *Interim Provisions for the Management of the Computer Information Network Construction for the National Courts (for trial implementation).* This event marks the starting point of informatization of courts.

The years from 2002 to 2012 were a period of overall promotion of the work. In 2002 the Supreme People's Court convened a conference on the informatization in Shandong, at which a leading group was set up for the information construction, having thus reinforced the administration of the work. In June of 2007, the Supreme People's Court distributed *The Supreme People's Court Decision on Overall Promoting the Informatization of the People's Courts* which specified the guiding principles for the court information and made specific arrangements for its security mechanism. In this period, the Supreme People's Court also distributed a series of regulations, plans, technical specifications, basic requirements and implementation schemes for the construction work, and assigned it as the main task in the court reform. As a result, courts at all levels made it a priority to integrate both hardware and software. Investment in hardware has been moving forward from regular facilities of traditional database and servers to diverse court trial devices and video media. Along with an increased investment in hardware, greater efforts were made in the development and application of the software for case management, judicial statistics, decision making support, profile management and judge administration. In an integrated construction and application, with the former motivating the latter and the latter in turn promoting the former, using the computer information network is becoming increasingly important. And finally, more intense attention has been paid to the role of the informatization in enhancing the efficiency, supervision, and transparency of trials.

Ever since the Eighteenth National Congress of the CPC and particularly the Fourth Plenary Session of the Eighteenth Central Committee which strongly promoted a law-based society with the goal of the people's courts securing fairness and justice in every case for the people, court informatization has entered into a new era of strategic development, and has at the same time been facing new challenges and opportunities. The Supreme People's Court has made this mission a foremost priority and attached great importance to its fundamentals, wholeness and strategic necessity. The Supreme People's Court also stressed that without informatization, there would be no modernization of the courts, nor would there be modernization of the trial system, let alone judicial fairness and justice for the people. The courts of all levels are therefore expected to work hard to satisfy the increasingly diverse needs of the people, by implementing information technology in the entire process of judicial adjudication, enforcement, and administration. They are also expected to take full advantage of information technology in order to ensure good control of judicial routines and more efficient trials. Through high-level integration of information and trial, trial procedures and enforcement are to be reconstructed and the trial mode is to be reformed, by which all aspects of trial are to be recorded and real time superintendence effected so that overall standardization of judicial conduct is achieved.

The Supreme People's Court has always placed emphasis on the status and function of the information system in the courts, having issued a series of regulations and documents providing main technological specifications and criteria. And enforced application has obtained excellent results. And the courts of all levels, fully aware of its importance, have been speeding up their construction of the information system.

In December 2013, the Supreme People's Court published *A Five-Year Development Plan for the Information Construction of the People's Courts (2013-2017)*, and in 2015 successively put forward were *A Five-Year Development Plan for the Information Construction of the People's Courts (2016-2020)* and *A Five-Year Development Plan for the Information Construction of the Supreme People's Court (2016-2020)*, which have established guiding ideas, fundamental principles, development strategies, construction goals, key missions and guarantee mechanisms for the information construction over the next five years. In addition, *The Supreme People's Court on Overall Deepening the Reform of the People's Courts — An Outline of the Fourth Five-Year Reform of the People's Courts (SPC No. 3 of 2015)* (shortened to *Reform Outline* hereafter), as a programmatic document for judicial reform, also requires that the courts of all levels accomplish by means of modern information technology the various goals of reform, of which thirty-five (sixty-five in total) tasks are more or less dependent on information technology. "Promoting information construction of the people's courts" is both one of the important missions of judicial reform and the crucial engine and powerful impetus for the reform. It is also required that the "Tianping Project" be sped up, integrating the resources available and impelling various applied information in service of the courts and public needs, and a 100%, 95% and 85% information coverage be achieved respectively for the main practice of the high, intermediate, and lower level courts. Moreover, the *Reform Outline* requires the establishment of a mechanism, as of exercising trial and superintendence,for keeping record of all processes, mutual superintendence, and mutual checks, and promotion of electronic service based on information technology. As for the reform of judicial statistics, the *Reform Outline* explicitly proposes to establish a "National Big Data Center for Judicial Information". In addition, *Several Observations of the Supreme People's Court on Consolidating the People's Courts' Practice in the New Situation (SPC NO. 21 of 2014)* also makes "promoting information construction" an important part of consolidation of the courts' practice.

In 2015, Chinese courts upgraded the information system to version 2.0 of its interconnection and interoperability, upon the completion of its infrastructure; and with growing maturity of its kernel application system, initial success has been achieved in the collection and integration, as well as management, of judicial information resources and in constant improvement of the guarantee system. As a result, online case filing, online case handling and online office work, have been basically achieved in over 3500 courts; and a primary framework has come into being in which real-time data statistics, live updating, digitization and various trial work are in positive interaction, to the great advancement of the judicial practice in fairness and justice for the people. The information network thus constructed interconnecting the four-tier courts of the country is playing an increasingly important role in the state governance system.

During the years between 2013 and 2015, the Supreme People's Court held a nation-wide conference every year on the court information, clarifying the guiding principles and specific assignments for the work. In July 2015 at a symposium attended by the Chief Justices of the high courts of the whole country, it was pointed out that judicial reform and informatization are as important to the people's justice as "the wheels to a vehicle and the wings to a bird", and required that the courts of all levels, while being fully aware of the role of informatization in the big data era, reinforce their sense of responsibility, mission, and urgency, and be intensely devoted to transforming and upgrading informatization to version 3.0 with distinct Chinese characteristics.

Contents

1. The theoretical foundation and practical significance of court informatization 1
1.1 The theoretical foundation 1
1.1.1 Need for facilities 1
1.1.2 Orientation of services 2
1.1.3 Construction costs 2
1.1.4 System risks 2
1.1.5 External circumstances 3
1.2 The practical significance 3
1.2.1 Serving the people and safeguarding judicial justice 3
1.2.2 Reinforcing judicial transparency and standardizing power enforcement 4
1.2.3 Optimizing judicial administration and enhancing trial quality and efficiency 4
1.2.4 Adapting to social changes and serving the state strategy 5

2. Achievements in the court informatization construction 6
2.1 A full coverage of courts in a rapid network construction 6
2.1.1 Information networks for trials and administrations at the Supreme People's Court 6
2.1.2 Information management platforms at the local courts 10
2.2 Judiciary Measure innovations to serve the people 12
2.2.1 People enjoy "less running about, less spending, and less trouble" 12
2.2.2 No more "hard to be served" and "hard to be interviewed" 14
2.2.3 Keeping clear the passage for the public interest demands and complaint articulation 15
2.2.4 "Legal services delivered to the door" 16
2.2.5 Keeping a "micro" distance in the aid of new media with the people 17
2.3 Informatization assisting in the modernization of trial capability 17
2.3.1 Constructing technological courtrooms 18
2.3.2 Implementing long-distance video system 20
2.3.3 Electronic courts online 20
2.3.4 The court e-stamp and e-signature 21

2.4 Significant enhancement of the court enforcement capability and effective credit corrections 22
2.4.1 Current construction and working of the information management system at the Supreme People's Court 23
2.4.2 Current construction and working of the information management system at the local courts of various levels 24
2.5 Precise management of trials and dynamic monitoring of their working 25
2.5.1 Enhancing the trial and enforcement quality and efficiency 26
2.5.2 Providing smart services for the judges 27
2.5.3 Optimizing and reconstructing the procedure of trial and enforcement 29
2.5.4 Monitoring the situation and serving the trial and enforcement 31
2.6 Deepening judicial openness and contributing to the reinforcement of the court public credibility 31
2.6.1 Informatization promoting open trial process 32
2.6.2 Informatization facilitating open ruling documents 34
2.6.3 Informatization deepening open enforcement information 35
2.7 The judicial reform gaining its momentum by information technology 37
2.7.1 Informatization promoting the reform of trial and enforcement 37
2.7.2 Informatization boosting reforming judicial management 38
2.8 Concentrating big data to enhance governance 40
2.8.1 Accomplishments in concentrated management of judicial information 41
2.8.2 Big data in service of socioeconomic construction 43
2.9 Boosting the construction of honest and clean courts and supervising judicial power exercising 44
2.9.1 An application system for discipline inspection and supervision 44
2.9.2 Easy access of complaints and reporting 45
2.9.3 Improving the internal supervision and monitoring system 45
2.10 Information construction in steady progress and the guarantee mechanism in constant improvement 46
2.10.1 Organization leadership and team construction 46
2.10.2 Maintenance guarantee and information safety 46

3. The direction of future work 48
3.1 Upgrading conception and revolutionizing the judicial system with informatization 50
3.2 Making top-level design for an overall coordinated advancement of the court information system 51
3.3 Mastering judicial regularities for an in-depth coalescence of IT and court operations 59
3.4 Balancing supply and demand and assisting in trial enforcement in service of the people 60
3.5 Improving data analysis and serviceability for a better service to socioeconomic development 63
3.6 Strengthening team construction for training and exchange of excellent specialists in the court information 65

Concluding remarks 66

Appendixes 1: A list of the official documents for the informatization of the country-wide courts 67

Appendixes 2: A Five-Year Development Plan for the Construction of the Information System of the People's Courts (2016-2020) 72

1. The theoretical foundation and practical significance of court informatization

1.1 The theoretical foundation

A lot of things in human society are accomplished by communication of information. So far altogether four transformations in communication mechanisms and modes occurred in history, namely oral, written, printing and electronic communication. And in the whole process of such transformation technological revolution served as a major impetus. Likewise the electronic technology, which is instrumental to electronic transformation of mankind communication, has led human society into an information era, in which information has become an extremely important production force beside land, labor force and capital. To meet the challenges of the information age, General Office of the CPC Central Committee and General Office of the State Council jointly issued in 2006 *Development Strategy for National Informatization from 2006 to 2020*, which brings forward development strategy of China's informatization, and requires that information technology be fully adopted in exploitation of information resources and prompts bolstering information exchange and knowledge sharing, improving the quality of economic growth, and driving forward socioeconomic transformation. And in the wave of information age, the court informatization has already become one important component of the national informatization, with its primary goal being to realize and enhance judicial justice and credibility by way of boosting the modernization of trial system and circumstances.

The court informatization does not simply mean a transformation of trial and administration modes, but is a system engineering involving a whole battery of judicial practices in trial, personnel and administration affairs, of which five areas are to be specially attended to: needs for facilities, orientation of service, construction costs, system risks, and external circumstances.

1.1.1 Need for facilities

The construction of the court information system consists of a network and its infrastructure, system software and application software, data resources and hardware terminals, which make up the basic framework of the information engineering. In the construction of the network and its infrastructure, a clear logical relationship needs to be appropriately constructed between the court intranet and the internet as well as the government network, and accordingly the mode of data transmission between networks and safety control of data storage need to be designed from information safety perspective. In software development, an upgrading system needs to be effected to keep pace with the development of information technology and the progress of modernization of the court practice, and to provide more quality services for judicial trials. The hardware is the key link connecting the judicial staff with the computer data center, and the informatization of courts is mainly targeted to various types of data resources produced in the process of judicial practice, including texts, pictures, and audio-visual materials, in the light of which the hardware terminals are supposed to be capable of handling different data types. While processing diverse data, an uniformity of data format should also be secured. Diverse terminals such as computers, cameras, and scanners need to adopt uniform format criteria in data collection and transformation, enabling smooth transmission and compatibility of data between equipment and networks, so that a big data archive can be constructed, free from fragmentary information and "information-isolated island".

1.1.2 Orientation of services

Along with the deepening reform come about dramatic social changes and increasing demands for justice from the public. The kernel objective of the court informatization is to implement justice for the people and meet the diversifying demands of the people. To achieve the goal the informatization needs to closely combine the court administration system and trial practice and work toward an organic unity of informatization and to the goals of practical efficacy and satisfaction of people's needs.

Further development in the court informatization will definitely reduce the costs of social communication, accommodate the needs of the information age, and be more responsive to social needs; it is instrumental to raising the courts' capability in data collection and processing, optimizing trial procedures, and improving judicial competence, so that the law optimally matches the ongoing reform.

1.1.3 Construction costs

Since the courts are the main undertakers of the court information system, it is therefore advisable to investigate and evaluate information construction with due consideration of its practicality for the courts. In most of the courts, disparities exist in the light of their administration and technological capacities across different regions and levels, hence their costs of information construction vary to some extent. So the courts are supposed to conduct cost evaluation of their own technological capacity and general situation before making feasible planning for information construction.

The court information construction being a long term process of investment should be embedded into the existent established organization and administration system and subject to constant convergence, upgrading and transformation, and in the process significant costs are entitled. For instance, in digitization of the original paper documents thus produced from trials and enforcement, a lot of labor has to be devoted to system transformation, data input and storage, to which necessary investment has to be devoted in the initial stage of information construction.

1.1.4 System risks

Advanced technology prioritizes successful court information construction. However, apart from technology, mature and efficient administration is also a fundamental guarantee. Hence, the court informatization is not to concentrate on one at the expense of the other in terms of the "software and hardware". Here "software" means that in the process of informatization, both the courts and judges are faced with system risks such as changing of ideas and the need for improved ability in using information technology as well as coordination of various institutions within the courts, all of which can hardly be ignored. Another example is that the court routine information handling and decision making are more or less related to its administration and guarantee system. So if the court information construction affects the reform of trial administration and that of judiciary administration, corresponding "rejection" can be inevitable, thus incurring risks to the very construction.

1.1.5 External circumstances

As a system engineering, the court informatization simply cannot be accomplished separately from the external circumstances. Supportive forces from both the institutional soft circumstance, such as central policies and judicial reform, and from the physical hard circumstance, such as financial input, manning, and facility supply, are indispensable in the smooth promotion of the court informatization. Therefore the external circumstances ought to be mutually coordinated and boosted with the internal circumstance of the courts' information system to achieve a good atmosphere. Accordingly the courts should in the process of information construction be proactive in making public their achievements and highlighting the efficacy, and in sharing and interworking of data with other government institutions, while striving to form a positive cycle and to make greater progress in information construction.

1.2 The practical significance

In recent years the courts of the whole country have taken initiatives in accelerated informatization construction. The Supreme People's Court have decreed a series of documents, and made clear the general goal and cardinal direction for the court informatization. And in 2015, the Supreme People's Court once again stressed that the courts, while centering on a full promotion of the strategy of ruling the country by law and under the guidance of the *Reform Outline*, should strive to modernize the trial system and capability and speed up the construction of the court informatization system version 3.0 based on the big data. Through years of construction, the court informatization has displayed the following practical values.

1.2.1 Serving the people and safeguarding judicial justice

The court informatization has successfully promoted the modernization of the court practice, having highlighted the fundamental principle of justice for the people. In other words, the people's needs are the key orientation of the court information construction. On one hand, the information system has helped to reduce litigation costs.

The availability of the internet platforms such as government websites and mobile terminals have effectively boosted the communication capacities of the trial enforcement information and made it easily accessible to the public, having thus guaranteed to a great extent the people's right to know, right to participate, right to express and right to supervise. On the other hand, the courts have been able to take advantage of informatization in collecting huge amounts of judicial data, which have been highly supportive for the courts to acquire a reliable knowledge of the trial regularities, having thus efficiently boosted judicial quality, prevented miscarriages of justice, and safeguarded judicial justice. Moreover, sharing of data concerning country-wide legal cases has been made possible, and on the basis of which the courts of different regions have conducted data exchange, and by jointly reviewing and focusing analysis on certain types of cases effectuated judicial justice in the practice of reaching the "same verdicts in identical cases". While seeking guidance from the cases of the Supreme People's Court, the courts of different levels may also offer guidance and submit feed-back via databases to guarantee judicial uniformity and justice.

1.2.2 Reinforcing judicial transparency and standardizing power enforcement

Various openness mechanisms embedded in the court information system have secured the formation of "Courts in sunshine". The open information of the trial procedure enables the interested parties to be duly updated of such information as the progress and development of the trial, and the handling stage of the case at issue, and to make judgments concerning their own rights and obligations and on the legal risks facing themselves. The live broadcasting and recording of court trials, and in particular the live broadcasting on the platform of new media such as "microblog" (weibo), can meet the demands of the public for auditing, to the effect that a boost of judicial openness can be realized in both width and depth. The publication of ruling documents online as an important step to the openness of justice has laid a good foundation for strengthening instrument reasoning and standardizing the exercise of judicial power. It is optimal to intensify open information, such as informing the interested parties and enforcement applicants in particular of the node information of the enforcement procedure, disclosing to the public the information of the interested persons who refuse to perform the ruling subject to enforcement, holding online auction to prevent manipulation for the security of auction transparency, and eliminating to a maximum extent discretion in the process of enforcement. It is also obligatory to further the openness of reduced penalty and conditional releases and to secure the transparency of such cases. Along with the ongoing promotion of informatization in various parts of the court business, definite progress can prospectively be made in the openness of case filing, court trial, enforcement, auditing, documents and trial practice.

1.2.3. Optimizing judicial administration and enhancing trial quality and efficiency

Along with the rapid development of socioeconomic society and growing awareness of rights and right protection, an increasing number of cases have arisen, and, as a consequence, the courts of all levels lack the man power to handle such a large quantity of cases. Now that they are the last line of defense for safeguarding fairness and justice, the courts should never be the least negligent in any case. This requires the courts to keep improving their trial and service capability to keep up with the times.

The court trial practice is just like a production line, on which different departments, while performing their own functions, work together in a collaborated manner to finalize the court proceedings. And on such a line the court informatization enables the circulation and sharing of related information. The division of work of the court informatization falls into the informatization of trial, enforcement, personnel, office work, and of government affairs. And in this process productivity is thus secured with available technology, to accomplish better trial efficacy, more efficient court administration, and greater quality of case ruling.

1.2.4 Adapting to social changes and serving the state strategy

Informatization serves as a great impetus to social changes, due to the fact that increasing production, circulation, and sharing of information speed up the popularization of knowledge and circulation of ideas, thus resulting in conception renewal and social progress. One of the goals of the court information system has been to boost the absorptive and processing capability of information by courts. The court used to have most of its information stored in traditional archives and documents, as well as in the database resulted from data collection. In the informatization process, such traditional resources are transformed into electronic data for further categorization, collation and analysis to produce more valuable judiciary information. And it is with such digitized data and analysis that the courts are able to move forward to automation, networking, and "smart" courts to adapt to social changes.

The rising of China does not reside merely in a growth in her economic and military strength, but more importantly in the enhancement of her soft power and a command of the power of discourse and rule-making. In recent years the Party and the state put forward a series of national development strategies in deepening the reform and widening the opening, and for national big data, and innovation-driven development. And Informatization is an important path to the realization of these national strategies. Based on fast-growing information technology the internet is becoming a must-have in social management, production, and everyday life, interconnecting various social aspects. One of its advantages is its interconnection of miscellaneous information on a global scale, breaking the barriers of time and territorial geography. Nowadays in a rapid development of global knowledge economy and information, informatization is a crucial factor in improving the court practice, and an important path as well to communicating trial experiences across regions, industries and countries and promoting the Chinese judicial model. China is in her optimum time of development, and it is therefore essential for China to do her own work well, and to make her own contribution to mankind's judicial civilization with a successful formation of distinctive Chinese court theory, practice, experience and approach.

2. Achievements in the court informatization construction

During the "Twelfth Five-Year Plan", and particularly since the 18th Party Congress, because of the powerful reinforcement of the Supreme People's Court, the courts of all levels depending on the "Tianping Project"[1] have completed the court information system version 2.0 in terms of interconnection. Its main content is that an interconnecting and comprehensive information infrastructure has come into formation with the office intranet, the court network, the external networks, internet and secrecy-involving net being used as ties, of which altogether ten types of applications have provided direct support for judicial service, enforcement and judicial administration. Also taking shape are three types of information resources, with those of trial enforcement as the main body and including those of personnel and government affairs, for which integrated management of data has been achieved. The principal goal of justice for the people in information service has been made more explicit, and the judicial protection of human rights significantly improved.

2.1 A full coverage of courts in a rapid network construction

Remarkable accomplishments have been made in the court network and in its infrastructure construction since the initiation of the court informatization construction. By the end of 2015 the court network has practically covered the courts of four levels in the country, namely altogether 3,512 courts have realized networking and interconnection, having laid solid foundation of network for further implementation of information in various court practices.

2.1.1 Information networks for trials and administrations at the Supreme People's Court

The Supreme People's Court has constructed a series of national networks for trials and administration, including China Judicial Process Information Online, Chinese Judgments Online, Chinese Trial & Enforcement Information Online, and Chinese Court Live Broadcasting Online. These are the direct results of the court informatization.

1 "Tianping Project", literally balance project, shortened for "State Judicial Trial Information System Project", is an electronic government project, which was reported by the Supreme People's Court to the National Development and Reform Commission for approval and undertaken of its construction in collaboration with the people's courts of various levels across China. Its major content includes formulating standardization criteria, developing application software, improving network and storage environment, providing guarantee measures for trial support, monitoring and management, and system security, and constructing nationally unified judicial database.

China Judicial Process Information Online has been put into operation. It is a key to court openness, and an important path for the people to participate in lawsuits, and to secure the interested parties' litigation rights, as well as the people's right to know. In August of 2014, China Trial process online was put into operation. Based on the open website for trial procedures, eight types of node information were forwarded in a timely manner to the interested parties and legal representatives via mobile texting, voice phone system, WeChat, "microblog"ging, and mobile APPs, by which any updating of information of the case concerned would be on automatic push notification, having thus effected "whole dragon service" on behalf of the court.

"Chinese Judgments Online" has been in operation and kept upgraded. The ruling document is the final product of a court trial; it is an important document of the court's determination of facts, application of law and judgment, being thus the important text medium bearing all the way through litigation activities, settling of disputes, and the quality of judgment. Releasing ruling documents online has been a significant undertaking to deepen judicial openness, to display judicial civilization, and to safeguard judicial justice. Such documents are not only made accessible to the interested parties, but to the public at large, for social supervision and unification of justice standard, and for actual realization of fairness and justice in each case. These documents used to be extremely restricted in access, and one had to go to the hearing court to look up a specific document at the great expense of great time and energy. In November of 2013, the Supreme People's Court opened "Chinese Judgments Online", having henceforth concentrated the publication of the ruling documents subject to enforcement at all of the country-wide courts. The database of judgments has become an important component of Chinese Big Data of Justice. At the end of 2015, in an attempt to improve the user-friendliness of the website, the Supreme People's Court upgraded the network by adding to its homepage one-click smart queries on related documents, individualized service and minority languages sections. The successful networking of ruling documents has made easy access to the public for query and research on one hand, and on the other it has produced a wash-back effect, prompting the judges to enhance their reasoning ability for betterment of document quality and judicial practices.

The country-wide investigation and control system for networking enforcement has been completed. In the past few years, the court had aggravating and prevalent problems of "difficulties of enforcement", in that it was difficult to find the persons subject to enforcement, difficult to obtain the executed properties, difficult to seek assistant executors, and difficult to move executed properties, and with frequent interventions, hindrance, and resistance to enforcement. All these seriously held back the enforcement of court judgments. On December 24 of 2014, the Supreme People's Court opened up an enforcement commanding system, which on the basis of the information system undertakes joint actions of enforcement and concentrates administration of enforcement on a national scale. In order to realize country-wide networked investigation and control, the Supreme People's Court has established with the ministerial headquarters of joint actions the "General to General" investigation and control system. And accordingly, various high courts have established with the provincial headquarters of joint actions "point to point" investigation and control system, having thus actualized online investigation and control of the persons and properties subject to enforcement. By the end of December of 2015, the Supreme People's Court had opened up the "General to General" system to 3,172 local courts of various levels; and by using the system altogether 1,130,000 cases of queries had been conducted involving over 1,300,000 persons subject to enforcement, and over 1.9 trillion RMB yuan bank deposits under investigation, of which over 36.3 billion was frozen. All this has effectuated maximum protection of the legitimate rights and interests of the enforcement applicants and defended the judicial authority of the courts.

Live Video Broadcasting Network of court trials has been put in operation. The network has served as a convenient platform for the courts in the country, and it is at the same time an important coordinating measure in judicial openness, for which three great platforms have been developed for making public trial procedures, ruling documents and enforcement. On the platform there are currently several sections, such as "Live Court Hearings", "Live Previews" and "Live Reviews", through which all the high courts, intermediate courts and grass-roots courts throughout the country have had their trials broadcast online (so far altogether 130,000 court hearings have been broadcast online), so that people could review any previous trial on the "Live Reviews" section. The website also provides query service for people to view trials they are interested in. Now that the Chinese court live video broadcasting has been routinized, people can better exercise their rights to know, participate and supervise in the whole proceedings of court cases. Meanwhile the judges' speeches, rulings and behavior are further normalized, having thus realized multidimensional judicial openness and judicial fairness.

Lawyers Service Platform has been constructed. The Supreme People's Court has established Lawyers Service Platform and developed National Information Infrastructure for Lawyers thereupon, so as to provide convenient and efficient litigation services for lawyers in their performance of responsibilities. On the platform lawyers are able to get access to online filing, files, case information queries, electronic servicing and can contact judges online. Up to February of 2016, altogether 21,846 law firms, and 77,428 individual lawyers had made entries of their information into the database. Such a platform has been a great convenience for the lawyers to handle their cases and to communicate with the judges; and it has proved a remarkable success for safeguarding the lawyers' rights and interests.

Judicial Assistance Management Platform has been completed. On January 1, 2016 the platform was placed online and began its operation, which has not only improved the quality and efficacy of judicial assistance in case handling involving Hong Kong, Macao, Taiwan and foreign countries, but contributed to judicial cooperation between Chinese courts and their international counterparts. In a globalized world, it is a fact that crimes have become internationalized, with civil and commercial disputes being increasingly across regions and nations, for which international judicial assistance has become an important trend in international judicial cooperation, necessitating comprehensive judicial assistance and cooperation by all countries. Therefore the platform serves as an extensive linkage, in its effective realization of international judicial assistance and cooperation, interconnecting other countries and regions, while having extended the reach of the courts and broadened their scope of practice. Up to February 20, 2016, on the platform 51 cases of investigation involving Hong Kong, Macao and Taiwan had been done, together with 2 cases of investigation in foreign countries, 1,213 judicial documents serviced to the regions above, and 455 documents serviced to foreign countries.

An Appeal & Petition Management System has been completed. The Supreme People's Court has completed the online Appeal & Petition Platform and Petition Management System, so as to strengthen and improve the handling of petitions and legal actions. The system functions to handle incoming letters, visits, online litigation and petitions, long-distance video reception of visits and data sharing. In May 2014, the platform opened its long-distance video reception of visits, which is a significant step forward to deepening reform of the petition handling mechanism and to the stage whereby local petitioners could have face-to-face interactions with the judges of the Supreme People's Court in their own places. The Supreme People's Court have set up 17 sets of long-distance petition reception systems interconnecting their corresponding systems at the local courts for interaction and communication among the three parties, namely the Supreme People's Court, the court of first instance and the petitioners. And a petitioner can appeal and submit his or her documents to the court of first instance or other grass-roots courts of his or her residence. Accordingly, the court can also ask the interested persons to be interviewed via long-distance video reception when necessary. The combined actions of reception by way of long-distance video streaming system among the four levels of courts have provided a positive solution to the problems of petitions in that the petitioners no longer need to pay physical visits to Beijing, and to their other related difficult situations. In a complex social situation in which there are diversifying social interests, protruding social conflicts, and the fact that the judicial public credibility is called into question, the establishment and use of the petition management system together with the long-distance video petition reception system has effectively relieved the pressure of petitions related to legal actions.

Various court office and case handling platforms have been constructed. Depending on the informatization construction, the four levels of courts countrywide have initially released, on their private nets, authoritative documents and business communication with an integration of various applications. The two platforms for office business and for case handling have been upgraded in their convergent and expanding applications, having unified their working desktops and thoroughly connected to the systems of petition and IT supported courts. And on the platforms in wide practice have been wap push of legal regulations and typical cases, automatic generation of routine papers and documents, automatic typesetting of ruling documents, automatic error correction, automatic name covering processing before uploading online, automatic synchronous publishing of the trial processes, and one-click uploading and online publishing of the documents subject to enforcement. All these have further optimized the different function modules as of procedural examination and approval, management and control of power limits, and performance display.

The personnel information management system has been completed. Traditionally, the personnel information management of various courts worked in a separate and isolated manner, and resulted in delayed updating of personnel transfer information and inefficient management. Supported by the court informatization, the personnel information management system, having been designed to integrate personnel information and boot the national court personnel information management system construction, has served to carry out an overall management encompassing judge employment, job transition and transfer, job performance, personnel selection, commending and rewarding and other management tasks regarding judiciary profession personnel. Such a system is a realization of general informatization of the judges in the country and of analysis thereupon.

A micro platform has been opened up. Along with the construction of "China in broad band" and "Smart Cities" as well as the development and application of such new media as "microblog", WeChat, and News APPs, China is stepping into an era in which "everyone has a portable mic, and each carries a camera". The courts, making full use of the real-time interaction and participation on the new media, are expected to expand the channels as well as the extent of public participation to comprehensively receive public opinions and be more effectively subjected to public supervision, and explain judicial rulings in a timely manner and accurately register the public's concerns. For this purpose, the Supreme People's Court, taking advantage of the new media for quick dissemination to a large group of users, has opened up "microblog" and WeChat for the timely release of authoritative court information. And it is through such multi-channel, multi-dimensional, one-stop, and interactive openness, interaction and services that the courts are striving to produce a clear voice, transfer positive energy, and create a good image, and finally to increase public confidence in justice and effectively enhance judiciary public credibility and involve public participation and interaction. The Supreme People's Court has also initiated Chinese courts on mobile TV for real-time release of information. Across China nearly 3,300 courts have opened up official "microblog", having thus formed a "microblog"ging pattern of "national team + local team". Up to February 2, 2016, the number of participants in the "microblog" of the Supreme People's Court had reached 29.47 million, having released 18,239 pieces of "microblog"s, which had been forwarded 1.6 million times. The Supreme People's Court had released 822 issues of official Wechat, including 4,918 pieces of various information, with over 300,000 followers. And on Chinese courts on mobile TV altogether 4,005 clips of videos had been played, totaling 24,560 minutes in length, and with a sum total of 656,000 customers.

2.1.2 Information management platforms at the local courts

A full swing informatization has also been carried out at the local courts of different levels. About 99% of the courts countrywide have constructed office business net while joining the specialized court net, with a basic completion of the infrastructure as in network facilities, computers, storage hardware, and system software. About 47% of high courts have completed facilities or systems for non-confidential data isolation and exchange, and conducted data exchange across the nets such as between the specialized court net and external net as well as internet. While the video conference system has full coverage across the country, the systems of technology courts, long-distance arraignment, and long-distance reception of petition have achieved basic coverage of the countrywide courts, and some of them have even constructed their standardized computer centers and digital conference systems. About 21 high courts have constructed enforcement commanding centers, while 17 high courts have completed their information management centers.

By the end of 2015, the courts across China had all completed their own platforms of trial process information online and got them connected to China Trial Process Information Online. Henceforth, the release of the trial process information has essentially met the demands of the interested persons and legal representatives for queries thereof, having thus completely changed the old situation in which only the judges and clerks handling the case knew the information, and the interested persons had no means of knowing without asking somebody for assistance.

The courts across China have constructed or joined the government websites and judicial open platforms of their superior courts, and in some regions the internet applications have moved to a public cloud platform, with internet and various mobile applications gaining momentum, all having significantly contributed technologically to the services of the courts of all levels for the people. Up to February 2016, all the high courts across China, together with 358 intermediate courts and 2,747 grass-roots courts, had constructed their own websites.

The high courts have connected by using special network or local government network with the various state administrative institutions, properties, public finance, inspection and police, having initially met the demands for coordinated work in information reporting and sharing, executive investigation and control, and credit discipline. The high courts in Fujian, Guangdong, and Zhejiang provinces have constructed a "point-to-point" judicial investigation and control system, which, by joining up the databases of institutions such as police, industry and commerce, and state land property, has made possible multi-dimensional and concentrated acquisition of information concerning bank deposits, estate properties and vehicles of the executed, having thus relieved various difficulties of enforcement.

The high court in Shanghai opened up lawyers services platform at the beginning of 2015, on which about 1,325 lawyer's firms together with 17,000 lawyers thereof can enjoy easy service of "filing a case within the firm". One lawyer stated that such a platform "is not only conducive to a lawyer's case handling, but more importantly, it helps both the judges and lawyers to reach a common understanding of the case under examination. As legal workers, despite the fact that the judges and lawyers learned the same textbooks in university, they may have different perspectives of the same event due to their different roles. The present sharing of resources on the platform serves to push back the limits of their thinking and complete their knowledge of the case with the database, which is of great significance."[1]

The information of judges in Beijing and Shanghai has been put in association with that of cases on the platform for concentrated management of the court database, and based on which a performance profile of each judge can be generated, namely how many cases each judge handles yearly, and how many are remanded and overruled in the same year are clearly shown online. Thus the performance assessment based on such information is more reliable, authentic and therefore more convincing.

2.2 Judiciary Measure innovations to serve the people

The informatization of courts is of great importance to meet people's increasingly diverse needs for justice and to adapt to social transformations. With the support of information technology, the courts have opened up new areas and new windows of justice for the people providing better services for the public. In practice, a lot of courts have set up "three in one" litigation service centers integrating litigation reception hall, service network and 12368 hotline, providing for the public judiciary services online filing, electronic servicing, live broadcasting of trials, document queries, and litigation archive queries. Many courts have initially realized proactive disclosure of important information, real-time query and prompt reply to questions, having thus formed a diverse pattern of judiciary service as demonstrated in its availability both on-and-off line and inside and outside the courtrooms. And on account of all the above, the public can enjoy easier, cheaper and more individualized litigation services and come closer to full justice.

2.2.1 People enjoy "less running about, less spending, and less trouble"

The litigation services hall is a physical place established by the courts providing litigation-related services. It provides for the litigation participants litigation guide, filing registration, pre-trial mediation, fees collecting and refunding, queries and consultation, receipt and transfer of materials, and post-trial Q&A. The litigation services hall usually has separate sections for litigation guide, document writing, waiting, and filing, presenting litigation flowchart and *Litigator's Guide.*

In December, 2014, the Supreme People's Court, on the basis of "filing petition window", set up a multi-channel, one-stop, and integrated "three-in-one" litigation services center, which has multiple functions of its services for retrial filing, petition reception, information queries, and archive queries. At the center the litigators and the participants can make queries on the related cases and electronic archives using the touch screens and computers.

In December 2014, the Supreme People's Court opened up "litigation services

1 "Shanghai Court Lawyers Services Platform kicks off and lawyers can file a case online within the firm", retrieved February 21, 2016 from http://www.chinanews.com/fz/2015/01-05/6938108.shtml.

online", providing services for online filing, case queries, electronic servicing, online reading, and online supervision and suggestion submission. The interested persons can submit civil application documents for retrial, and the litigators can log on the net for queries concerning case progress. The platform also delivers the node information concerning the case procedure to the interested persons, agents and defenders via mobile texts, WeChat, and "microblog"ging.

On September 6, 2015, Beijing court litigation self-service platform was fully started. And on the platform the interested persons can enjoy one-stop service, including making reservations for archive reading, printing documents, submitting materials, and leaving video messages, covering all the steps of litigation. Different from traditional functional systems, the platform is designed to highlight personalization and humanity. Embedded in the platform is an intelligent recognition system, by which the interested person, by swiping his or her ID card, can get instant recognition, and get access to the display of information concerning the court date, trial judge, and ruling document. Another characteristic of the platform is its realization of cross-district services based on the concentrated trial database, thanks to which the interested person can print out his or her ruling document at home, and make queries on all kinds of information of the cases and trials undertaken by any court in Beijing; the interested person can keep track of the case handling, and leave video or voice messages, which the court and judge in turn can receive in real time and have interactive communication with the interested person. By the end of January of 2016, Beijing high court had set up 108 self-service litigation terminals at the 23 courts and 63 courtrooms in the city, having achieved a full coverage of all the courts and districts in the city. And during the time period from September 2015 to the end of January, 2016, the accumulated number of users of these terminals at Beijing reached 250,000 person time, among whom over 5,000 person times as of cross-district service. Such remarkable accomplishments have earned unanimous praise from the people.

In the process of a trial on a tourist contract dispute at Beijing Daxing district court, the plaintiff was required to present the liability report on the traffic accident in the process of tourist service but was unable to do so. The trial judge, having learned that Beijing Miyun district court had already had a trial on the transportation contract dispute over the same traffic accident, got contacted on the litigation services platform with Miyun district court for sharing of the required evidence. The acquisition of the evidence only took several minutes and saved a lot of time for the interested persons, who were amazed and said, "the 'one-stop service' has brought about 'one trial clear', it is really great!"[1]

In 2012, Nanjing intermediate court was the first to have constructed the litigation service center online on the internet in Jiangsu province and extended the functions of its physical litigation service center to the trial online of the courts at Nanjing. With its initial functions of the court online, people upon logging on the net are able to not only enjoy

---

1 See "Practically reducing the workload of the both the interested persons and lawyers; Beijing Daxing all-out forging 'service on finger tips'", *People's Court Daily*, November 29, 2015, 4th edition.

services, as they do at the physical litigation services center, for filing cases, signing for legal documents, submitting evidence materials, making appointments for an interview with the judge, and asking questions after trial, they can also obtain in time various kinds of node information concerning the trial proceeding and enforcement. Moreover, they can also apply for, for specific reasons, court hearing online and video reception. By the end of 2015, the page views had reached 214,000 person time, with various legal services having reached 32,182 person time.

By the end of November, 2015, altogether 1,740 litigation service centers together with 841 litigation service websites had been completed and opened. It is arguably true that the informatization has build up a bridge of communication between the courts, judges and the public, having provided quality and cost-effective litigation services, and in particular, saved a lot of travel and labor for litigators in remote areas, so that people have less rushing about, less spending, and less trouble.

2.2.2 No more "hard to be served" and "hard to be interviewed"

One of the biggest problems encountering the litigators used to be their finding it hard to be served at the court and hard to find the judge. The fact is that a judge was usually in charge of many cases and had a lot work to do, which is why the judge failed to be "present on call" in response to every specific interested person in each case. In order to clear the conduit linking the public and the courts, to provide a solution to the problem stated above, and at the same time to enhance the informatization of judicial services, twenty-five high courts across China set up the hotline 12368 system of litigation services in their jurisdictions, providing litigation services to the interested parties via voice phone and consultation services to the public in its later extension. The hotline is a comprehensive service platform integrating a battery of functions handling litigation consultation, case queries, petition and complaint, and contacting judges. Ever since it began operating, it has contributed a lot to relieving the workload of the judges, informing the litigators of the case progress, and providing judiciary services to the public.

In January 2014, Shanghai high court set up the hotline 12368 litigation service platform, of which the main functions include: assisting the interested parties, agents and other participants contacting via voice phone concerning judge filing, trial judge, and enforcement judge or providing voice message service; the interested parties can make queries, using a query code provided at the case filing, on legitimately disclosed information concerning whether the case is being handled, case number, trial or enforcement progress, court date, the responsible judge, work phone, and litigation material delivery; providing consultations on routine procedural questions such as regulations of case jurisdiction at the courts of different levels, the court-provided conditions for filing a case, regulations on collecting litigation fees, time limit of trials, and judicial reparation; receiving and recording petitions and complaints and forwarding them to the petition and complaint system for timely handling; receiving and recording the comments and suggestions to the courts or judges from the interested parties and the public and providing timely feed-back; an internal assessment is to be conducted on all the courts and judges by taking into account the comments and suggestions, petitions and complaints therefrom.

The hotline 12368 of judicial services in Zhejiang province has the same integration of different functions, while carrying out at the three levels of courts a working mechanism of "using one hotline to the public, making classifying arrangement, combining actions by all courts, and setting time limits for handling". The court has designated a hotline coordinator, who is in charge of receiving and handling incoming calls from the public.

2.2.3 Keeping clear the passage for the public interest demands and complaint articulation

The law and litigation-related petitions comprise a large proportion of the overall petitions. In order for the public to articulate their complaints, the Supreme People's Court opened up the appeal and petition online in February 2014, accepting cases dealt with according to law, including the cases in which the interested parties disagree with the effective judgment, ruling and decision specific to criminal, administrative, and state indemnity cases, and has already appealed to the high court, and to which the high court has produced a written review (investigation) or retrial conclusion, and those appeals and petitions for urging the court concerned for a prompt enforcement or for correcting executive behaviors. The platform adopts the mode of accepting from the internet, handling on the intranet, and providing replies on the internet, and in conformity with which the interested parties fill out their appeal or petition online, and submit the corresponding materials before completion. Upon submission, the interested parties can make queries anytime on the handling progress of and feed-back to their appeals and petitions.

To make sure that people know how to use and make good use of "Appeal and Petition Online", the Supreme People's Court has produced a guide to appeal and petition online and video clips of animation, explaining in detail each step of operation on the platform. Moreover, on the platform the disclosure of typical cases is further enhanced. The "appeal and petition online" has broadened passage to appeal and petition and innovated measures of justice for people's convenience. Along with the construction of the platform was also completed the long-distance petition video reception system. From the commencement of its operation in May 2014 to February 2016, 8,900 incoming video calls had been received on the platform. On account of the major adjustment and reform of the state policies on petition and of the implementation of the platform mentioned above, the number of groups and person-time of litigation-related visits to Beijing has reduced 30% from a year earlier.

The local courts of all levels have also positively promoted petition online. A large majority of the courts have set up long-distance video petition reception systems and appeal and petition online platforms, having provided convenience of services for appeal and petition. As an example, the courts at Gansu, while persisting in "internet + petition reception" and promoting long-distance video petition reception system, have set up the online system at 107 courts in the province. Up to July, 2015, Gansu high court had received petitioners on the video reception system for 560 person-time, among whom some were from Yunnan, Hunan and Shaanxi provinces.

In 2014, the courts of all levels at Xinjiang Production and Construction Corps received petitioners on the long-distance petition reception system for 300 person-time, taking up over 35% of the total; and such long-distance reception by way of explaining the law and analyzing the situation successfully persuaded 30% of interested parties to give up appealing and petitioning. Upon the completion of the long-distance video petition reception system, spatial distance is no longer an obstacle, having relieved the people of their trouble of traveling and enhanced the efficacy of the petition handling by the courts.

2.2.4 "Legal services delivered to the door"

In the gradual upgrading of the court informatization, the courts of all levels carry out justice for the people, and provide convenient and highly efficient legal services by introducing the "mobile court on vehicle".

The mobile court on vehicle employs the designated vehicle specifically designed for the courts to conduct circuit trials, which is actually a mobile digital court equipped with high technology for the purpose of providing convenient services to the people in the remote and border areas for litigation, on the spot trials, mediation of neighborhood disputes, offering legal consultation and carrying out legal system publicity. The mobile court has greatly extended the reach of the court and the judicial governance. The vehicle for the mobile court is usually equipped with an alarm lamp, a siren, an audio system, a power system with external interface, an uninterrupted power system, a power inverter for constant power supply, a video recording and live transfer system, as well as a table for trial.

The mobile court on vehicle has an important role to play particularly in undeveloped and remote areas. For instance, Ningxia high court has 63 local courts and nearly half of their jurisdictions are located in deep mountains, mountainous areas and middle arid areas with poor transportation connections. To solve the problem of litigation inconvenience, Ningxia was the first in the court system of the country to popularize "mobile court for convenience service", with each of the 63 courts being allocated a vehicle for mobile court, so as to enable the people to enjoy quick and convenient judicial services.

Such a mobile court on vehicle has expanded its functions in the practice. The district court of Jiangjin district of Chongqing was the first to have successfully developed an integrated multi-functional and all-weather court on vehicle of modern technology, which was put into operation on October 15, 2013, being capable of multiple tasks such as litigation services, circuit trial, legal publicity, enforcement commanding, and long-distance petition reception.

The mobile court on vehicle, adhering to the idea of "good tradition + high technology", and with its integration of litigation services, circuit trial, legal publicity, and video petition reception, is a modern and upgraded version of "Ma Xiwu Style"[1] trial service, and is warmly called by the people "legal services delivered to the door".

2.2.5 Keeping a "micro" distance in the aid of new media with the people

Using the new media to shorten the distance between the court and the public has been in recent years a new mode and new channel of innovative communication with the public initiated by the court. The courts countrywide, taking advantage of the real-time interaction and participation as prevailing in the new media such as mobile APPs, "microblog"ging, WeChat, and micro-videos, have made it possible and feasible as well for the interested parties to have real-time interaction with the court and obtain necessary information for ready communication.

By the end of 2013, the Supreme People's Court had fully stationed on the mainstream "microblog"ging platforms all over China, such as Sina "microblog", Tencent "microblog"ging, and the National Court "microblog"ging, on which a number of court hearings of great social consequence had been broadcast live on the Court "microblog"ging, in order to explain the law with the cases, spread the legal culture, enhance legal spirit, play the judicial role in social education, guiding and regulation, and simultaneously the court proactively exposes itself to public supervision and ensures that judicial officers are prompted to improve their capability and trial quality.

The Supreme People's Court has also opened official WeChat and mobile TV APP integrating various open channels to provide to the subscribers one-stop services of judicial openness and for public opinion communication. From the end of February, 2015, "Chinese courts on mobile TV APP" began to deliver first-time new highlights and judicial information concerning the court trials of the key cases.

An expanded application of information technology has been instrumental to innovations of the service measures of justice for the convenience and benefits of the people, while having significantly reduced judicial costs. And in the process of this, people are enabled to have more feeling of fairness and justice around them, whereas the court comes "micro" close to people on the new media.

2.3 Informatization assisting in the modernization of trial capability

Trial capability as a key embodiment of the court competence is the ability of the court to make just judgments according to law and to effectively safeguard fairness and justice, having the direct bearing on the realization of social justice. The modernization of trial system and capability finds expression in the standardization of judicial power

1 Ma Xiwu (1899-1962) was the presiding judge of East Gansu branch court under the jurisdiction of the high court of Shaanxi, Gansu and Ningxia border areas in the administration of the Communist Party of China. He always paid visits to villages, while carrying the case documents with him, for close investigation and held circuit trials and handled cases on the spot. His fairness and integrity as demonstrated in his performance of trial proved a great welcome to the ordinary people, henceforth the "Ma Xiwu Style" trial.

exercising, in the materialization of the supervision and management system, and in the technical support with information technology. And its ultimate aim is to serve the court trial and enforcement and judicial management and to meet the judicial demands of the court on one hand; on the other it is to serve the public and meet their judicial demands. The court has to improve its trial capability in accordance with judicial discipline, in its pursuit of judicial certainty, standardization and justice, by way of establishing a trial power exercising system centering on trial, and establishing trial supervision and management system centering on the judge accountability. In such a process of modernization the informatization of the court is a must-have, as it efficaciously keeps away and cuts down uncertainty,thus making the exercising of judicial power in conformity with the judicial discipline with lower costs for safeguarding social justice.

A trial is a central task of the people's court and one of the major concerns of the public at that. Since the public has a high expectation for trial hoping that the court makes fair judgment to its utmost extent, a relatively big tension is thus created between the public expectation and the practical judicial competence of the court, and such contradiction can be resolved to some extent by way of informatization. In another word, the information technology has significantly transformed the modes of trial and greatly boosted trail capability and efficiency. The case information management system is a realized digital management of the major procedural node information and archives, enabling programmed operation of trial tasks and being conducive to the standardization and supervision of the exercising of trial and enforcement power. And the trial supporting system provides services in which the judges can make queries on laws and regulations, obtain instructions on specific cases and references to measurement of penalty, and conduct one-click editing with smart error correction, thus making the handling of case more convenient and efficient and greatly enhancing the quality and efficiency of trial. In addition, e-signature and long-distance court hearing system has provided great convenience to both the judges and the public and reduced the litigation cost and judicial cost. Informatization has become an important component, so to speak, of the trial capability. All over the country more than 99% courts have completed their own case information management systems and successfully realized case handling online. Likewise, remarkable achievements have also been made in the construction of technological courtrooms, long-distance video system, and electronic courts.

2.3.1 Constructing technological courtrooms

The courts countrywide have made vigorous efforts in the construction of technological courtrooms, carrying out synchronous audio and video recordings for the whole process of trial procedures, concentrated data storage, regular backup, and long-term or period-specified retention. Up to the end of 2015, the courts across China had completed construction of 18,000 technological courtrooms. A number of courts had achieved remarkable accomplishments in expanding the coverage of these high-tech courtrooms. At the courts in Jiangsu 2,279 technological courtrooms had been constructed, having realized whole-process synchronous audio and video recordings of the case proceedings, synchronous records and display of the records. In Zhejiang province all the 1,783 courtrooms had been turned into technological ones and realized all-time recordings of trials. In Guangxi Zhuang Autonomous Region 293 courtrooms had realized a full technological coverage, while having all joined up the court audio and video management platform at Guangxi and carried out synchronous recordings of trials. In Xinjiang Uyhur Autonomous Region 115 technological courtrooms had been constructed with the function of long-distance arraignment, with each of the courts having one such courtroom.

The people's courts of different levels adopts technological courtroom, which, by making use of multi-media display of evidence, recording of cross-examination and of trial, strengthens the process of proof-providing, cross-examination, and authentication, ensuring that the court trial is not just going through the motions by implementing the practice that everything takes place on the spot of the court hearing: providing litigation evidence, presenting plea and defensive arguments, conducting debate making clear distinction between rights and wrongs, examining facts, and forming juridical reasons. In addition, the real-time audio and video records provides support and guarantee for the panel discussion, the trial commission deliberation, and the playback of the court hearing at the retrial as well as for the observation and viewing of the case by related institutions and the public.

The whole-process synchronous audio and video recording enables "frame-positioning", "playback", and "duplication" of the court trial, thus strengthening the whole-process supervision and all-round management while enforcing the standardization of trial and enhancing the first-time success rate of trial. The Jixi district court of Jixi city, Heilongjiang Province, had its first-time success rate of trial significantly raised during the time period from June of 2013 to December 2015: that of the civil cases raised from 70% to 86%, that of the criminal cases from 89% to 95%, and that of the administrative cases from 86% to 94%.

The whole-process synchronous audio and video recording, in its actual record and authentic retention of the speech and behavior of the judge and litigation participants in the process of the court hearing, can be used on one hand to conduct effective supervision on the judicial performance of the judge for trial standardization, case handling in accordance with laws, and safeguarding the litigators' rights, and on the other it serves to constrain the behavior of both the plaintiffs and defendant, providing evidence for the recognition of their possible disturbance of the court order, which is also a protective measure for the judicial personnel. In recent years the interested parties occasionally had irrational behaviors; and there has been an increase in the violation of the court order, like assaulting the court, abusing the judge, and damaging evidence, imposing threats against the personal safety of the judge. Yet little punishment had been affixed to such misbehavior, due to one fact that there was a lack of valid evidence for the recognition of a disturbance. However, the whole-process synchronous video record serves to make up for the traditional manual record and computer keyboarding, with its frame-positioning and playback functions providing strong evidence for recognizing a disturbance of the court order. It can be seen that the technology has double-layered functions: it imposes standardization of people's behavior while safeguarding their rights; it is conducive to the supervision of the judge while constraining the behavior of the interested parties.

2.3.2 Implementing long-distance video system

In a widening application and constant innovation as well have been the long-distance trial, and arraignment online. By the end of 2015, ten sets of such system had been constructed at the Supreme People's Court, and 2,154 sets at the local courts, having thus realized long-distance arraignment among the Supreme People's Court, various high courts, intermediate courts, and a large majority of grass-roots courts as well as a number of houses of detention.

In a first cross-province long-distance case trial, the plaintiff attended the trial at the high court of Liaoning Province, whilst the defendant appeared in the court at the intermediate court of Zunyi, Guizhou Province. The event saved for the plaintiff over 10,000 RMB yuan as would have been spent on food, hotel accommodation and trips. As the plaintiff said after the trial, "the long-distance trial saved both my time and energy, and I didn't have to travel so far as to Guizhou for safeguarding my legal rights."

The court of Qingtian county, Lishui city, Zhejiang Province tried to set up the court online dealing with the lawsuits of overseas Chinese, which, by making use of long-distance video for court hearing, is able to connect the video camera on the computer desktop of the interested party abroad to the high definition digital court, so that the interested party on the other end can attend the trial on a computer or mobile APP. Such an endeavor provides a solution to the overseas Chinese in different countries attending the court trial in China. Since 2014, at the court of Wenliang city, Zhejiang, out of the 3,763 concluded criminal cases there have been 2,984 cases under summary procedures, and of which 1,542 have been finalized on the long-distance video trial, taking up about 51.7% of the total summary procedure cases. The average session time of the video trial has been reduced to 15 minutes, and the rate of pronouncement of judgment at court has reached 95.6%, having saved of police manpower 1,600 person-time in contrast with the regular escorting and court guarding.

The long-distance trial has been an important innovative measure in the service of justice for the people's convenience, having saved a lot of troubles on the part of the litigators and shortened the trial cycle, enhanced the trial efficacy, and lowered the judicial cost.

2.3.3 Electronic courts online

An electronic court is the working direction of the court informatization. In 2015, Jilin electronic court was formally opened up online, having realized the whole-process online handling of the civil cases of the first and second instance, administrative cases, enforcement and non-litigation cases. Together with the electronic court was constructed the judge assistance platform, which effectively mitigated the workload of the judges and brought down the risk of making different determinations on similar cases to guarantee judicial justice. Moreover, the electronic court at Jilin also developed trial management system to carry out real-time assessment of the judge's performance and the quality and efficacy of the trial. As its subsystem, the case proceeding management system had real-time display of the case filing and handling of each judge at each court of the whole province, thus enabling the trial quality and efficacy assessment system to conduct real-time assessment of each judge at each court.

The electronic court greatly shortens the average cycle of the case trial with the efficiency of the judge's case accepting and handling being significantly improved. First, it ensure a case filing within the legally designated term. The different parties of litigation can submit and transfer their materials online, pay fees online and have electronic servicing, and in combination with the real-time reminding message from the 12368 hotline, the interested parties can have their case filing within the specified time period without frequenting the court for providing additional materials. Second, it shortens the term of the court session. The different parties of litigation use online exchange and cross-examination of evidence, cloud conference platform, hearing, prosecuting and defending platform, and online court trial, so as to enjoy longer valid time of hearing, longer time of pre-court preparation and opinion presentation; whereas the court can have quicker determination of the disputed issue and carry out trial and mediation around the issue and is capable of concluding the case within the legally normal term. One example is a civil case on trial at the court of Jiaohe city, Jilin Province, on which the plaintiff and defendant, having uploaded 31 pieces of evidence on a third party platform, upon online cross-examining of the evidence, had disputes over 6 pieces of them, on which the collegial panel investigated and checked at the hearing and came to an affirmation within 30 minutes, given the fact that such case used to take at least half a day for court hearing. So the trial quality and efficacy has been significantly enhanced. On account of the fact that the whole process of the court trial was made open and transparent to the public, and that the disputed issues were made clear, and long-distance mediation was conducted via cloud conference, the success rate of mediation, the rate of lawsuit withdrawal, the rate of acceptance of the first instance judgment and that of cessation of appeal all had been increased; the number of applications for enforcement went down after mediation, thus having significantly enhanced the trial quality and efficacy. Finally, realized was the guarantee of the lawyers' various rights. The electronic court platform provides for the lawyers windows handling their individual represented cases, and lawyers dynamic tokens, having thus greatly facilitated the lawyers' participation of the trial.

2.3.4 The court e-stamp and e-signature

For each case more than ten types of legal documents are produced by average from filing to conclusion. And the courtrooms at the township are usually more than ten kilometers or even dozens of kilometers away from the grass-roots courts, so there has always been the "difficulty of acquiring stamps". Usually the legal documents are sent by specially designated person and vehicle to the court acquiring stamps, while the interested parties are required to collect them at the court at a notified time. Such a process not only consumes large volume of manpower and material resources and adds to the burden the interested parties, but seriously affects the efficiency of the case handling.

With the support of information technology and by adopting e-signature, the problem mentioned above can be fundamentally addressed. By applying e-signature, the mediation agreement and statement of decision can be immediately delivered upon mediation and withdrawal of appeal. And for the pronouncement of judgment at court, the verdict can be collected "instantly in a waiting time", significantly enhancing the efficiency of case handling, making the interested parties free from the troubles of trips coming and going to the court, and reducing their litigation costs. Suppose the interested parties on each case reduce two trips to the court, approximately one day time, then each case can save over 80 RMB yuan of the litigation cost. Accordingly, suppose the working staff of the courtroom reduces 5 trips to the court on each case, which approximates half a day, the judicial cost for each case is reduced by average over 100 RMB yuan. More importantly, the social and legal benefits arising therefrom greatly surpass the economic benefits in terms of figures. The court of Jiangxian county, Luzhou city, Sichuan Province, combined the trial judge accountability system with e-signature, and as the result of which the judge in charge was able to apply e-signature before printing out immediately upon the completion of the judgment document and deliver the documents to the interested parties at the first time, while it is a fact that such a procedure would have taken the judge several days to finish before.

The e-signature has also been widely used in the office work and case handling at the courts. A synergy of online office with the e-signature system effectively shortens the time limit of case handling and enhances its efficiency while reducing the judicial cost. Initial success has been achieved, in the constant advancing implementation of informatization, network and technology in the courts, in the enhancement of justice for the people and fair justice, in increasing people's satisfaction, and in building judicial credibility.

2.4 Significant enhancement of the court enforcement capability and effective credit corrections

Enforcement is an important work of courts and an important link in implementing the rights and obligations as provided in the effective legal documents, being at the same time the "last kilometer" in guaranteeing the rights of the interested parties. Therefore it has direct bearing on not only the realization of social fairness and justice, but the authority of judicial adjudication, and is thus pivotal to promoting judicial credibility. In actuality many judgments had been difficult to be executed due to various factors, having done serious harm to the judicial authority. And among the various attributing factors the major ones were difficulties in finding out the property under investigation and the persons subject to enforcement. In the past it used to be the practice in which two judges traveled on a car all the way round trying to find out the property and persons for enforcing a verdict, which can no longer meet the demands of the new period for enforcement. A new way of thinking has to be adopted to extend the reach and innovate the means of enforcement; and it is the very place the court informatization comes into play. In recent years the enforcement information application system has been established at the courts all over the country, covering all the kernel procedures of enforcement, such as commanding system, enforcement information management system, and credit correction measures.

2.4.1 Current construction and working of the information management system at the Supreme People's Court

In December 2014, the Supreme People's Court set up a national enforcement commanding system, having realized both vertical interconnections among the enforcement networks at the four level courts all over the country, and horizontal abutting joint connecting some of the central state institutions and the head offices of commercial banks. A hierarchical and joint-action enforcement commanding system at the four level courts has come into formation, with the Supreme People's Court, the majority of high courts, a number of intermediate courts and grass-roots courts having each constructed enforcement commanding systems, enforcement control and credit correction systems.

The enforcement information management system is of six major functions as of network check and control, information disclosure, credit correction, long-distance commanding, supervision management and decision analysis. The network check and control enables queries with high efficiency on the deposit information of the persons subject to enforcement at over 3,000 bank outlets. And the enforcement commanding system enables "one-click" affirmation by looking into how much property the person subject to enforcement is in possession of and whether the person is hiding it in refusal of enforcement. On the platform the executives at the four level courts all over the country are all entitled to exercise check and control on the debtors' identity and properties.

The Supreme People's Court has also disclosed "black lists" of those dishonest persons subjected to enforcement, having thus produced a strong deterrent effect on the dishonest behavior.

With the support of information technology, the administrative judges have fundamentally transformed their modes of enforcement and thus enhanced their efficiency, and yet with which has also come along a growing hazard. To curb the "abuse of public power" and prevent the disclosure of the citizen's privacy, the courts have established a multi-layer system guarantee mechanism. For example, the official letter of assistance in enforcement from a court must be double-verified by the court and the bank to confirm that its invoked activity is in conformity with the law. Meanwhile, the commanding system also keeps record of the "whole-process traces", which automatically records and offers reminder on the judge behavior in the whole process, making visible whether a judge positively exercises check and control and whether he or she has misbehavior.

2.4.2 Current construction and working of the information management system at the local courts of various levels

The local courts of various levels have been exploring both in width and depth an extended implementation of informatization. The high court at Beijing has constructed the enforcement and commanding management system integrating all the courts of the city, which, with the support of information technology and by embedding into the platform standardized requirements for the procedure and time limit of enforcement, has effectively regulated the practices on over 130 nodes of 4 main categories such as prompting and reminding, approving management, supervising and urging, and procedure controlling. The commanding system at Beijing classifies the cases into property-involving and non-property-involving categories, exercising on the former procedural operations and node controlling, and on the latter carrying out dynamic management on a separate database. In addition, an intensive query mode has been set up at Beijing for a great enhancement of the efficiency and effect of the enforcement, having of its query function covered all the 86 banks at Beijing, and of its integrated query and freezing function and automatic queries on real estates, household, and vehicles effectuated at 9 commercial banks. In 2015, the courts of the whole city executed and concluded 122,929 cases, which rose 19% from a year earlier; and the underlying assets thereof amounted to 60.74 billion RMB yuan, which rose 96% from a year earlier. A unified management system for executed money has been constructed at the three-level courts of the city, having concentrated and unified management of money receiving and dispatching at different courts, which used to be under discrete management, and carried out fine management by way of "setting up one account for each case". Such an endeavor serves as a solution to the problem in which the sources of money in the process of enforcement always got unidentified and money dispatching or returning always got delayed, thus reducing the corruption risk on the part of the administrative judge. Moreover, a visual display platform for enforcement has been established, on which set up are over 5,400 indicators for analysis, thus providing for the enforcement commanding institutions at the courts of various levels multi-layer, multi-perspective and multi-dimensional dynamic information of enforcement. It also provides more specific references for decision-making in optimizing the enforcement standardization and innovating the enforcement management modes.

The courts at Zhejiang have set up long-distance enforcement commanding management system and related it to the case information of the enforcement and case handling system on the court private net, sending back the real-time case handling information collected on the mobile devices by the administrative judges to the long-distance visual commanding and coordinating platform at the enforcement departments. And the enforcement commanding system serves to coordinate, through commanding vehicles, individual devices, and enforcement recording instruments, frontline police officers and the commanding offices at the various courts to enhance collaborated enforcement among the courts and to improve their quick response capability. The courts at Zhejiang have also set up unified long-distance enforcement conferencing system, which serves as a visual communication platform interconnecting the commanding centers of various levels or the commanding offices at the grass-roots courts for real-time multi-consultation on the court private net.

The intermediate courts at Shenzhen has established an eagle-eye check and control net interconnecting and interacting via the net with the joint-action departments, carrying out check and control on the persons subject to enforcement and their properties. The eagle-eye check and control net has its major functionality in exercising check and control on the executed person's bank deposits, real estates, vehicles, equity and stocks. The administrative judge at each court submits the request to the eagle-eye check and control net before it delivers the requested information to the assistance department, which in turn feeds back the results upon the completion of the task. The eagle-eye check and control system claims the following advantages: First, it has saved a lot of manpower. The check and control work that used to be done by 54 persons at the two-level courts at Shenzhen can be done by only 5 persons now. Second, it has spared a large quantity of facilities. In the past what had to be done by going out with over 20 vehicles can be done by delivering online the request to the assistance departments. Third, it has shortened the cycle of enforcement. What had to be done for 15 working days can be done within 2 days by now. Fourth, it has added new categories of properties for check and control, having expanded to 28 from 4 categories. Fifth, it has greatly extended the scope of property checking. By linking up to the enforcement commanding system of the high court at Guangdong, on the platform the checking of the executed property can be carried out beyond Shenzhen and extended to the whole province, with the checking of the executece persons' bank account, stocks and funds being conducted all over the country.

2.5 Precise management of trials and dynamic monitoring of their working

The trial management as an important component of trial is of three factors, namely procedural management, quality monitoring, and performance assessment. The procedural management is targeted at the node information in the trial proceeding. Traditionally, the management of the cases at the courts had long been carried out by hand-kept standing books and judicial statistical forms with little guarantee of the reliability and accuracy of data and no timely reflection of the dynamic condition of the trial on focus, still less conducive to discovering the problems as arose in and improving the quality and efficacy of the trial process. Particularly in recent years there has been an explosive growth of the cases accepted by the courts and an increasing workload of trial and enforcement, and along with which there have been a growing demands for justice and diversifying evaluation on the trial effect. As the consequence of such changes the traditional mode of trial management with judicial statistical forms as the major means has its drawbacks revealed more and more prominently. Such practical condition and the public demands requires adopting new technology and new modes, and in response to which comes into play the mechanism of trial and enforcement information management implementing the idea and method of big data, having become itself an important task of the court informatization.

2.5.1 Enhancing the trial and enforcement quality and efficiency

The quality and efficiency of trial and enforcement is the foundation of just judicature; and information technology has a great role to play in trial management and the improvement of its quality and efficiency. The various information network systems and litigation services platforms are the important carriers of online office work, filing, case handling, querying, and appealing, and the technological supporters for the court trial and enforcement. Taking the court trial closing as an example, quite a number of courts across the country had the problem in the yearly case handling of "being slack at the beginning and having to speed up towards the end" and the malpractice of applying "a screeching halt" onto new case acceptance at the end of the year[1]. In 2015, due to the downturn of economy, reform of case-filing register system, introduction of judicial interpretation on civil procedural law and modification of administrative procedural law, there was an abrupt increase of new cases at the courts across the country. In order to deal with the problem, the Supreme People's Court issued *Urgent Notification on Further Strengthening Law Enforcement and Case Handling* requiring the courts of all levels to concentrate on trial and enforcement. Meanwhile the Supreme People's Court, with the support of database system, carried out research and judgment on the operation of trials, offered timely notification of the general information, consolidated tracking supervision, and balanced the case handling tasks by shunting the caseloads in terms of the amount of workload at each trial department. In the beginning of 2015, the Supreme People's Court made a summarization of the trial work of the court for the year 2014, and henceforth produced for each quarter *Report of Situation Analysis on the Trial Operation*, providing data support for various institutions and judges for them to master the overall situation, to make clear where problems and gaps lie and to positively carry forward their work.

At a great number of local courts also set up was the performance quality and efficiency evaluation system. At each court in Beijing a special trial management office was set up, undertaking over 10 functions such as information collection, problem research and judgment, offering suggestions to decision making and process monitoring, and providing references to the leaders at all levels for their decision making by regularly collecting, analyzing and releasing evaluative data reflecting the trial quality and efficiency and by regularly compiling and distributing notifications on the trial management. In addition, a meticulous trial quality evaluation system with 35 targets in 4 classes was established covering all the courts, all the trial courtrooms, all the judges and cases, so that each court, courtroom and judge could proactively find out the existent problems in the light of the specific targets, and take corresponding actions to solve them.

1 Under the pressure of "year-end closing rate" as a criterion for yearly performance assessment, the courts used to be reluctant to accept new case filing at the end of the year to get around the short time lapse for closing a case.

At the courts of Zhejiang two quality and efficiency evaluation systems respectively on trial and enforcement were set up, carrying out via the data center automatic data collection and computation of the synchronously input information and automatically real-time generating 26 evaluation targets for case handling, which was the first of its kind in China, so that each court could see clearly its own strengths and weaknesses as well as its rank place and gap in contrast with all the courts in the province, having thus greatly improved the informatization of case handling management. The system is also of flexible functions in performing data tracking monitoring, forewarning, retrieving and statistic, which is capable of auto-prompting and keeping off missing recording and wrong recording and of tracing back the procedural information on each node of each case, having realized scientific quantitative management of each judge at each court, and enhanced the pertinence, objectivity, and authority of the evaluation thereupon.

The Fourth Intermediate People's Court at Chongqing, relying on the "case handling system online", designed and developed "trial management synthetic system software", incorporating five components of "judge's performance evaluation", "judge's quality and efficiency evaluation", "management of case assessment and measurement", "case information management" and "department work evaluation". The system not only serves to quantify a judge's trial work performance, and to enable the administrator to make structural adjustment through data on the trial resources to their optimal allocation, but also provides a platform for the presiding judge to exercise his or her power of trial management and supervision, having thus transformed the traditional mode of management within the courts. The visual ized whole-process supervision management has successfully ruled out the harmful intervewing factors to the trial practice and kept track of the supervisions conducted by the presiding judge, which is conducive to implementing judicial accountability and investigating into misjudged cases. Moreover, the auto-collection of trial data has enhanced an intensive and precise management of the court trials.

2.5.2 Providing smart services for the judges

The informatization provides technological support for the judges in their querying on and referencing to homogeneous cases, while ensuring their fact-finding and correct application of laws, reducing the uncertainty and subjectivity of the judicial adjudication and decision making, and promoting a unified adjudication criterion. It provides support for a dynamic management in assisting allocation of cases, adjustment of case points, professional panel discussion, having thus enabled the judge's to handle his or her case more conveniently and efficiently, the litigators to have their lawsuit better facilitated, and the justice to come closer to the public.

The courts at Shanghai developed altogether 35 software systems, including "Smart Assistance to the Judge's Case Handling", "Smart Analysis of the ruling documents", "Mobile Smart Case Handling APP", "Auto-generation of Legal Documents" and "One-click Office and Case Handling", to mention just a few, having thus realized for the judges smart case handling. The smart assistance to the judge's case handling by using big data analysis takes initiative in its push service of the information concerning related cases, reference cases and laws and regulations, thus providing for the judge's case handling individualized, precise and smart services. The smart analysis of the ruling documents system, by using big data analysis and judgment on the 61 quality factors of the ruling documents, can find out problems such as logic deficiencies and missing litigation requests and require the judge to make discrimination and correction. The system has made an accumulated analysis on 1.3 million ruling documents. The mobile smart case handling APP provides convenience for the judge in his or her handling of cases, reminder of on-going cases, case information query, and looking up trial documents, making the case handling more convenient and efficient. The widening application of the smart assistance to the judge's case handling system has enhanced to a great extent the trial quality and efficiency. In the year of 2015, a total number of 622,900 cases of different types were accepted at the courts of Shanghai, of which 614,500 were closed, with the closing rate rising 12.7% from a year earlier under the condition that the overall number of accepted cases rose 13.2%.

The First Intermediate People's Court at Tianjin developed a new generation platform with an integration of the court work, information and management, providing for all the police officers smart individualized public information service, duty function service and communication and interaction service, having thus realized embedded management, innovation of services and wisdom sharing. The first of its major functions is to provide smart and individualized information service, pushing case reference information, auto-recognizing the judge identity and specific case, and pushing to the judge as reference the collected, filtered and integrated relevant legal provisions, exemplar cases and the case-related public opinions. Moreover, it also provides trial procedural information, placing into 12 numbered modules on the homepage 12 major procedural information nodes concerning the court sessions on the queue, waiting for renewal of preservation, approaching time limit of trial and so on, and reminding the judge of the progress for an overall arrangement. Its second function is to supervise and urge the standardization of the judicial behavior. The platform has integrated the case management system, technical court system, document correction system, electronic archive system, and trial handling assistance system, embedded the various norms and standards regulating each node of the trial and enforcement process and placed trial management in its service, thus providing standard and guidelines for the court trials. On each node the judge can start a conversation discussing the case under examination, of which the whole process from the reminder of the court session to closing and archiving is in circulation on the platform for real-time viewing; and it keeps track of behavior and supports reversed query. All this serves to enhance the standardization of law enforcement. Its third function is collaborated construction and sharing of the judges' group wisdom. Various forums relating to different areas of trial, such as "Enforcement in Accordance with Law", "People Have No Small Matters", and "Problematic Cases" were set up for the judges, who are free to participate for sharing their experiences and conducting academic discussions to the effect of mutual enhancement. The individual experiences of the judges are pooled into collective wisdom, bringing about an overall improvement of the general judicial capability and promotion of an accumulation, sharing and sustainable development of the court information asset. Its fourth function is to enhance the efficacy of the judicial administration. The platform serves to enhance the administrative efficacy by integrating the administrative office system, putting together various administrative office sub-systems of official documents, information, vehicle management, facility maintenance, attendance management and instant communication for one-click login.

The intermediate people's courts at Nanjing of Jiangsu Province developed a mobile case handling platform "Smart Trial APP" and officially put into use in November of 2015. On the platform people can make instant queries on the litigation case handling, submit to the judge required materials, ask questions and put forward a reminder. Likewise, the judges can also directly handle the case, by using the platform on their mobile phone or tablet PC, instantly receive the submitted materials and answer the questions. In this way, a judge can handle a case anytime anywhere.

2.5.3 Optimizing and reconstructing the procedure of trial and enforcement

The informatization has transformed the traditional forms and promoted scientific management of trial management. It has reconstructed the trial and enforcement procedure and realized synchronous collection of the case information. At the moment the trial and enforcement personnel complete each task, the emergent litigation materials are input into the system, with all the information being completed of its acquisition on the same day of the work being done and the time of collection being automatically recorded in the system. And the paper documents such as the statement of claim, proof of evidence and certificates of evidence are to be scanned before uploading onto the system, while the electronic documents such as trial record and legal documents are instantly uploaded onto the system. Meanwhile, such judicial activities as the court hearing, identification, evaluation, auction, and preservation are also included in the information collection, while all the trials are being real-time monitored and video recorded in the whole process.

In 2015, the Supreme People's Court endeavored to optimize the case handling platform and add to the richness of its functionality in terms of assisting and facilitating the judge's case handling, while being oriented to the standardization of the trial management. As a result, many powerful functions can be carried out on the platform, including automatic synchronous disclosing of the trial process information, one-click online releasing of effective documents, process approving, managing and controlling of trial terms, and displaying performance, having basically realized the objectives of on-platform operating or synchronous uploading of the various documents as are produced in the course of case handling, including records of file review, trial reports, trial records, records of panel discussion, and ruling documents. A new working mechanism has initially come into formation in the management of case circulation online, online approving, whole-process synchronous monitoring and whole-process track recording, with the overall efficiency having been enhanced in enforcement and case handling by the means of modern technology.

The courts at Beijing have established a sophisticated system of the case process and formulated a dozen of documents regulating the management of trial process, trial term, court session, and archiving in terms of informatization, having realized effective monitoring of case filing, trial, enforcement, and petition through the optimization of trial process and precise node management.

The high court of Jiangsu Province has developed a digital trial supporting system with an integration of various software applications and built up digital courts through a unified user management, single sign-on, data sharing and business interaction. First, the system allows individualized setup of performance process. The new system supports individualized setup of special interfaces in terms of the roles and duties of the judge and assistants, on which the judge undertakes writing trial report and ruling documents while the assistants undertake data input and other routine work, having effectively enhanced performance efficiency. Second, it is to reduce the management nodes of trial process. Adopting new ideas the high court of Jiangsu transformed "process monitoring and controlling" into "process service", and reduced the number of management nodes from 42 to 6, including case filing, division of cases, changes of trial term, case conclusion, archiving, and transfer to the higher court of appeals, while the information of all the rest nodes is to be automatically collected with computer software. On the same interface are conducted different tasks, such as file review, trial, discussion, document writing, document servicing, case conclusion and archiving, and document release online, with an on-click generation of all the documents. The trial information is on a smart push. The high courts thereof also constructed the database of trial resources, integrating miscellaneous data resources such as the judicial documents, ruling documents, exemplar cases, and guidelines for homogeneous case trial. In the course of the judge performing a court hearing, the system can push to the judge, specifically to the case concerned, the related laws and regulations, judicial interpretation, exemplar cases, and document templates, while enabling relevancy searching and instant positioning. Third is the development of mobile case handling system. On the 4G private net, a judge can get access, via his or her mobile phone or notebook, to the uploaded materials from the interested parties, handle trial term changes, review and sign legal documents, view the video recording of the court trial, inquire case acceptance and conclusion, and handle case closing, thus enhancing the trial and enforcement efficiency.

The courts at Shanghai developed 45 systems concerning "trial and enforcement process management", "synthetic management of trials", "secretarial service management", and "personnel management", to mention just a few. The trial and enforcement management system performs audio and video recording and logging of the overall 450 key links of case filing, division of cases, court session, case closing and enforcement, and is a realization of whole-process visibility and through-track recording of the case handling while adopting E-stamp and E-signature. The executed money management system serves for visualized recond the whole process of executed money collecting, dispatching and returning. Up to the end of May, 2015, the courts across Shanghai had collected executed money 128.9 billion RMB, and of which 120.3 billion had been dispatched for 603,981 cases involved, thus presenting a straightforward display of the information thereof. All these systems have effectuated visualized management of the courts and plugged up the loopholes in the management.

2.5.4 Monitoring the situation and serving the trial and enforcement

An accurate judicial data statistics is of essential significance. To guarantee such accuracy and implement the transition from traditional manual statistic forms to their auto-generation on the system, the Supreme People's Court issued *Survey Schedules for Judicial Statistic Data Sources*, and selected 10 high courts at Beijing, Shanghai and other provinces as the experimental areas for informatization of judicial statistics in the year of 2015. Up to October 15, 2015, automatic generation of judicial statistics had been effectuated at 13 high courts in China.

An initial success has been achieved in the judicial data management and topical analysis service. Up to the end of 2015, the data centralization management platform at the Supreme People's Court had gathered altogether data entries of 70 million cases all over the country for the past five years. And currently the platform can automatically collect case data from 31 high courts across China at a five minutes interval and dynamically display the situation of case acceptance. Such data are of two practical uses. First, the court, by making use of technology, can acquire a reliable knowledge and mastery of trial patterns by analyzing huge complex judicial data, while conducting accurate fact-finding, correctly applying the law, and maximally reducing the uncertainty and subjectivity as is arising in the course of judicial judgment and decision making, to the effect of an enhancement of administration of justice and prevention of miscarriage of justice. Second, the court can carry out data mining, associating and analyzing of the cases at different stages, trial quality and efficiency, hot cases, and special types of cases, so as to get a command of the trial dynamics, tendency and internal pattern and better serve the judicial decision making and trial management.

The courts at Shandong Province established "Cloud Data Service Center for Shandong Courts", carrying out concentrated storage of various types of data and research and development of applications thereof. At the center the data of all the major businesses are real-time generated and updated every minute, together with auto-generation of 59 sets of basic and summary tables in 6 categories at the three-level courts, which are compared and contrasted regularly with the general judicial statistic report, thus presenting a "dynamic experience" for the trial and enforcement work.

The data operation situation analysis system has completed 18,000 groups of analytic figures and tables, conducting regular study and determination on the trial operation.

2.6 Deepening judicial openness and contributing to the reinforcement of the court public credibility

"Justice is to be not only realized, but in a visible way." In the rapid progress of legal construction, the public has an increasing expectation for the judicial openness and transparency. In December 2009, the Supreme People's Court stipulated *Six Regulations on the Judicial Openness*, requiring the courts of various levels to implement in their trial work openness in disclosing case filing, court hearing, enforcement, evidential hearing, documents, and trial practice. Recent years have seen a constant growth in richness of the open content, frequent innovations of ways, and continuous consummation of the mechanism. In November 2013, the *Decision of the Central Committee of the Communist Party of China on Some Major Issues Concerning Comprehensively Deepening the Reform* historically includes judicial openness in its statement:

> We will have more open trials, make the procuratorial work more transparent, and record and keep all court files. We will increase the persuasiveness of legal instruments and press ahead with publicizing court ruling documents that have come into effect.

The Fourth Plenary Session of the Eighteenth National Congress of CPC put forward deepening judicial openness and constructing open, dynamic, transparent and people-convenient judicial mechanism in sunshine. On November 28, 2013, the Supreme People's Court issued *Several Considerations on Promoting Judicial Openness in Constructing Three Platforms*, requiring promoting openness of the trial process, ruling documents and enforcement information.

The Supreme People's Court has constructed three open information platforms respectively for trial process, ruling documents and enforcement, while the courts of all levels having endeavored to adopt new media such as websites, "microblog"ging, WeChat, and Mobile TV and expanded mobile services thereupon. With the support of the three open platforms and the court new media, the courts across China have made coordinated planning for synchronously promoting judicial openness by expanding both its depth and width, having thus met the diversifying demands of the public for the justice and guaranteed the people's rights to know, participate, express, and supervise, while enabling the people to get hold of more authentic and comprehensive information and to feel the benefits of the judicial information openness, to the overall effect of an organic unification of both the social effect and legal effect of the case handling.

2.6.1 Informatization promoting open trial process

Open trial process as an important component of judicial openness is an effective solution to the interested parties' possible questioning of the justice of the trial when they have no timely access to the information of the trial process, and is also an important way by which the people could feel the fairness and justice in each legal case. The "Chinese trial process information online" at the Supreme People's Court timely delivers the following information: the first are the basic information of the court and its personnel, and that of condition for filing a case and legal fare charging standard; the second is the case filing-related information concerning the case filing title, registration number, data of filing, jurisdiction objection, property preservation, and advanced enforcement; the third is the trial personnel-related information concerning the board members on the collegial panel, court clerks, office phone, and ranks of the judges; the fourth is the trial-related information concerning the summons, notice of a court session, hearing of witnesses, records of the trial, and records of questions; the fifth is the evaluation and identification-related information, such as that of the name of an intermediary organ; the sixth is the trial guiding information, such as that of exemplar cases and illustrative cases; the seventh is the judgment-related information concerning, for example, the start time of servicing of ruling documents, the ending time of servicing, and that of manners of servicing; the eighth is the ruling document-disclosing information concerning the ruling documents, time of publishing, and the mode of inquiry. Up to February 20, 2016, on the Chinese trial process information online had been published, at the Supreme People's Court, 2,520 items of court session notice, and 258,000 items of trial information, with total visits having reached 888,500 and altogether 27,387 short messages successfully pushed.

The courts of various levels have also vigorously promoted constructing the platform of trial process information online. All the high courts have constructed in their jurisdiction unified platforms of the trial process information online linked to Chinese trial process information online. The completion of the trial process information online across China has primarily satisfied the demands of the interested parties and agents ad litem for queries of the case information. Since July 1, 2014, the interested parties have been able to conduct real-time queries on 93 items of 5 categories of information, on Beijing trial process online, concerning case filing, trial, enforcement, trial term, and case conclusion,[1] which can also be done on the mobile APP. The courts at Chongqing have printed on the filing notice and acceptance notice two-dimensional code, which the interested parties can conduct real-time query on the node information of the trial process by scanning.

The intermediate courts at Nanjing constructed online appointment booking for auditing, making public on the internet the arrangements of the court sessions on each day of the next week, so that the people could choose their interested case for auditing through appointment online. Over 15,000 person time had audited the court sessions through online appointment. And apart from that, the courts also invited 250,768 persons to sit in the court sessions of 40,058 cases, having collected 4,388 pieces of suggestions.

The platforms of trial process information online as constructed at the courts of various levels have primarily satisfied the demands of the interested parties and agents ad litem for the information of trial process. Nowadays people can get to know from online query who is in charge of the case and in what progress the case is being handled, while the short messages can be automatically pushed to the interested parties. All the trial activities are performed in the sunshine from case filing to judgment making, having thus guaranteed the interested parties' right to know and strengthened the transparency of the

1 The Judicial Reform Office of the Supreme People's Court, *The Judicial Openness of Chinese Courts*, The People's Court Press, 2015.

trial performance.

2.6.2 Informatization facilitating open ruling documents

The ruling document is the concentrated reflection and finalized product of the whole trial, and is the final result of the court's making clear of the fact finding and implementing applicable law as well as the key documents determining the allocation of the rights and obligations of the interested parties. Making public the ruling documents in accordance with the law in an accurate, all-round, timely and effective manner, and enabling the participants of the litigation and the public to be convinced of the judgment, is therefore a necessary requirement for a visible realization of judicial justice while enforcing the courts to improve their judicial trials. On the unified open information platform "China Judgments Online" hosted by the Supreme People's Court, the courts of various levels across China have had their effective ruling documents released in succession. Up to February 29, 2016, altogether more than 15,707,000 effective ruling documents had been released, with an addition of 40,000 pieces every day and including those in Uygur, Mongolian, Tibetan, Korean, and Kazakh, while the total views having reached 478 million clicks with an average daily views of 580,000 clicks. Having realized "full coverage of all types of cases of all the courts across China" (see Fig. 1), "China Judgments Online" is now the biggest of its kind in the world. And thanks to the incremental release of the documents online, the people no longer need to pay physical visit to the specific court for the related documents, but instead obtain them easily by logging onto "China Judgments Online". Many of the functions as provided on the platform such as advanced search, quick search association, streamline guiding tree, table of contents, one-click sharing, reading by two-dimensional code scanning on the mobile phone have all proved a great welcome.[1]

In promoting openning ruling documents, the Supreme People's Court stipulated special regulations, specifying the scope of document types that are not to be released online upon an intensified approving procedure, requiring that all the released documents be technically processed so that the people's personal privacy is properly protected.

1 "China Judgments Online in intelligent upgrading and four highlights on test|iCourt", retrieved February 23, 2016 from http://chuansong.me/n/2042740.

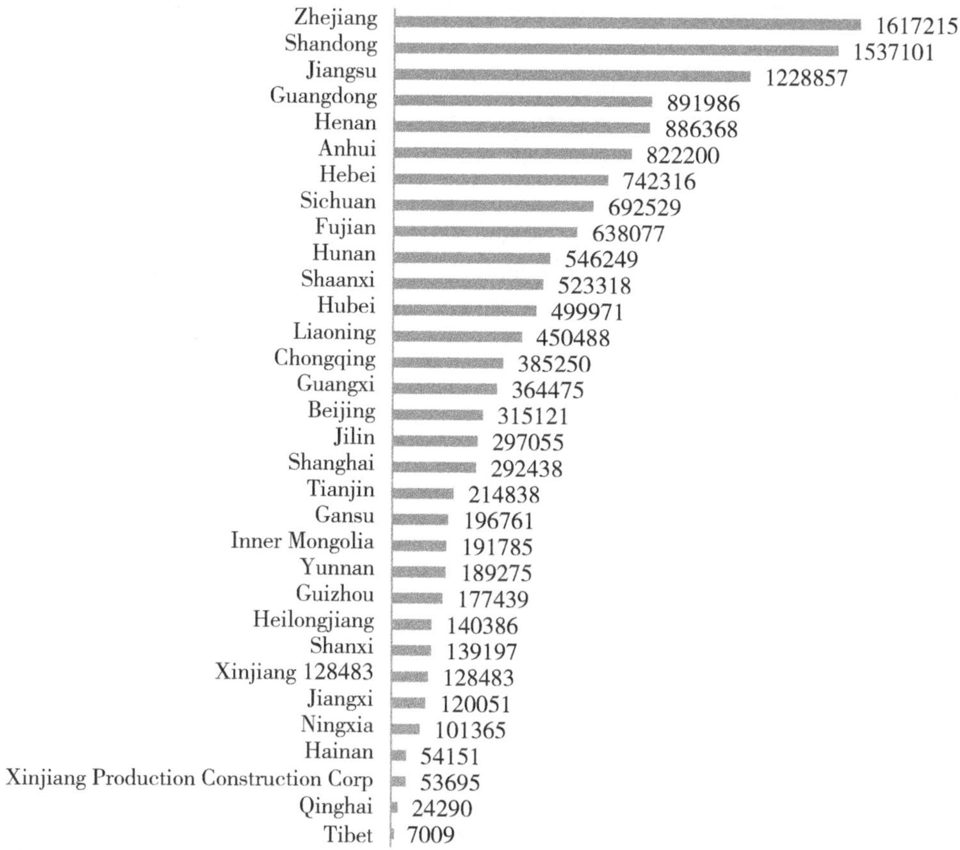

Fig. 1: Number of the ruling documents released online at some major provinces, municipalities and regions
Data source: China Judgments Online, retrieved June 22, 2016.

2.6.3 Informatization deepening open enforcement information

The enforcement work indicates the activity in which the court puts into practice what is finalized in the effective legal document in accordance with the law and upon the application of the interested parties. It is the last gateway of guarantee of the interested parties' rights and implementation of the judicial judgments, and is therefore of key importance to improving judicial credibility.

Open enforcement is an important component of judicial openness. The Supreme People's Court has constructed "China Enforcement Process Information Online", making public enforcement-related information to the interested parties and the pubic, and proactively accepting their supervision. On the platform is mainly released the information concerning case enforcement, name lists of the dishonest persons subject to enforcement, the persons subject to enforcement, and the ruling documents for enforcement.

The interested parties can obtain, by using their ID number and password, from the platform information concerning enforcement filing, executives, changes of enforcement process, enforcement measures, disposal of the executed property, enforcement of the judgment, settlement of enforcement, allocation of executed money, stay of enforcement, suspension of enforcement and termination of enforcement. And the public can also make queries on the platform on the information concerning the criterion for case filing, the disposition of the executed property and the notice of auction sale. Up to the end of 2015, on the platform altogether 37.66 million clicks queries had been made on the enforcement information.

The Supreme People's Court has established the system of disclosing the name list of the dishonest persons subject to enforcement, opening up the platform for "Disclosing and Searching of the Name List of the Dishonest Persons subject to enforcement at Chinese Courts" and "Black list of dishonest persons subject to enforcement" on the "microblog"ging and WeChat, while bringing out in collaboration with the People's Net "Rank list of Dishonest Persons Subject to Enforcement" for a wider distribution of information of the dishonest persons subject to enforcement, having thus formed a powerful credit disciplinary deterrence for enforcing the persons subject to enforcement to proactively perform their obligations. In December 2014, the Supreme People's Court also set up a commanding system for a unified management of all the enforcement cases at the courts countrywide, exercising finding out and controlling of the persons subject to enforcement and their properties and exercising punishment of the dishonest persons subject to enforcement.

The courts of various levels, by making use of the information disclosed on the platform and sharing the name list of the dishonest persons subject to enforcement with the related institutions, places restrictions for the persons subject to enforcement on their leaving the country, on bidding, and high consumption. In the course of practices above, the courts of various levels take active part in boosting constructing the social credit information system and constructing the networked finding and controlling system covering the information of all the dishonest persons subject to enforcement in China, reporting the name list of the dishonest persons subject to enforcement to the related institutions for placing restrictions on their purchasing of soft sleeper tickets and flight tickets, on their applying for loans and credit card, and for banning their acting as the legal person or senior administrator of an enterprise, thus enforcing the persons subject to enforcement to proactively perform their obligations. Up to February 29, 2016, altogether 3.02 million dishonest persons subject to enforcement had been disclosed of their information, with 40.11 million person time queries having been made on the platform. As for the collaborated punishment of the dishonest persons subject to enforcement in terms of the restrictions on departure, flight riding, and home starter loans, more than 3.88 million person time had been prohibited from purchasing flight tickets, and 780,000 person time had been prohibited from purchasing train tickets. The participating institutions and industries in collaborated dishonest punishment have extended from the initial 8 institutions such as China TravelSky Holding Company and China Railway Corporation to 19 institutions such as the Credit Reference Center, the People's Bank of China, while the scope of disciplinary punishment having been expanded from actual social activities to the virtual space on the internet.

2.7 The judicial reform gaining its momentum by information technology

The court informatization is not only an effective approach to integrating resources, enhancing efficiency, and reducing the workload of the judicial personnel, but also a major initiative to promoting judicial reform. Pushing forward the court informatization is one of the fundamental components in deepening the judicial reform, as modern information technology comes in assisting the courts to solve the practical problems and development problems arising therefrom.

The Supreme People's Court issued the *Outline of the Fourth Five-Year Reform Plan*, bringing forward 65 judicial reform measures covering 7 broad areas, of which the highlights being 1) establishing a judicial jurisdiction system that is appropriately separated from the administrative divisions; 2) establishing a trial-centered litigation system; 3) optimizing the internal disposition of function and power of courts; 4) improving the operation of trial functions; 5) establishing an open, dynamic, transparent and people-convenient judicial system in the sunshine; 6) promoting the normalization, specialization, and professionalization of the court personnel; and 7) ensuring the lawful, independent and fair use of judicial authority by the people courts. Of the 65 measures as included in the 7 areas stated above at least 35 measures are directly dependent on the use of technology, which is to be discussed in the following two categories.

2.7.1 Informatization promoting the reform of trial and enforcement

Many of the measures of trial and enforcement reform as brought forward in the *Outline of the Fourth Five-Year Reform Plan* are closely related to the court informatization, such as establishing an audio and video recording mechanism of the whole process of trial, reforming the system of case acceptance, improving the case division system, improving the trial grade system, improving the case quality evaluation system, deepening judicial statistic reform, deepening the enforcement system reform, and promoting ruling document argumentation reform.

"Establishing the whole-process audio and video recording mechanism of trial" requires the courts to set up the audio and video recording mechanism of trials, and imposes higher standard on the normalized operation thereof. The normalization management of trial recording has to be based on a viable mechanism for audio and video recording of trials, to promoting which the court informatization is a most important precondition and enforcement guarantee. In such process, the coverage of technical courts needs to be expanded on one hand, to upgrade the audio and video recording rate of trials ensuring track records and transparency of the whole process of trials; and on the other the quality of such recordings needs to be enhanced in terms of their higher resolution, on account of the fact that such mechanism not only serves judicial openness, but also serves the court work itself. For instance, the courts at Zhejiang reformed their way of trial recording, in the process of informatization, and explored to fully rely on the audio and video recording and to standardize trial process without employing court clerks for manual recording, having thus greatly saved time and manpower.

"Improving the case acceptance system" requires changing the traditional case filing review system into registration system, and increasing publishing online the filing information, which is of crucial importance to the completeness and accuracy of the open platform at courts. It also requires improving the supporting mechanism, including the diverse disputes settlement mechanism, pre-court preparatory process and case filing service. Among them the case filing service has bearing on the construction of the court litigation service center and its informatization. It is for the convenience of the litigators practicing their right to appeal to promote online case filing, making appointment for filing, and circuit filing. In 2015, the courts of Jiangsu Province accepted via online case filing registration 25,779 applications, of which 19,939 were registered for case filing, with the filing registration rate having reached 77.35%.

"Improving the case division system" focuses on a random division of cases. "Improving the case quality evaluation system" puts forward "with the support of the three open platforms respectively for trial process, ruling documents and enforcement information, giving full scope to the service, study and judge and guiding functions for the judicial justice of courts."

As for the enforcement practice, the *Outline of the Fourth Five-Year Reform Plan* puts forward requirements for "enforcement system reform", laying emphasis on establishing, specific to the dishonest persons subject to enforcement, a system of credit supervision, deterrence and disciplinary punishment, and on strengthening the reform of judicial auction measures by concentrating on online judicial auction. Currently, online judicial auction has two modes in China. First, in collaboration with the Taobao net it is to carry out judicial auction on its designated platform. Second, it is to carry online judicial auction on the litigation assets net at the court. The introduction of a third trading platform into online judicial auction serves to physically isolate possible interest associations by adopting electronic bidding online, thus making judicial auction operating in sunshine. Such an innovative mode is directly dependent on the informatization progress of courts, urging the courts to make new innovations and improvements in the process thereof.

The service provision system reform focuses on the new mode of electronic servicing, and on upgrading its efficiency and accuracy. While most of the courts were still considering electronic servicing via short message and email, it had been actually implemented at Zhejiang, Guangdong and other places, having not only created convenience for the interested parties, but saved judicial resources and enhanced service efficiency at that.

The above-mentioned measures have to be carried out on the basis of the court informatization platform and its effective operation and technical support. The higher version the court informatization gets upgraded to, the more it boosts judicial reform.

2.7.2 Informatization boosting reforming judicial management

Judicial reform is not only targeted at a more fair, just, open and transparent judicial practice, but at a more scientific and efficient judicial administration; this is an important approach to saving judicial resources and improving judicial efficiency. And because of this, a scientific reform is necessarily to be carried out on the court internal administrative decision making, administrative management, archive management, personnel management, disciplinary inspection and procuratorial work as well as on information management. Closely related with the court informatization are a series of measures of judicial management as put forward in the *Outline of the Fourth Five-Year Reform Plan*, including "promoting reforming the system of classified management of the court personnel", "improving the president and the presiding judge's trial management mechanism", "improving the court and judge's trial supervision mechanism", "improving trial management system", "promoting reforming unified management of the personnel at the lower-level courts below the provincial court", "straightening up the management relations of judicial administrative affairs of courts", "establishing specified number of judge posts system", "improving the judge performance evaluation system" and "improving in-service judge training mechanism".

"Improving the president and the presiding judge's trial management mechanism" aims to establish an internal supervision and check mechanism on the exercising the power of trial by the hearing judge and collegial panel and the president and presiding judge. Whereas, "establishing specified number of judge posts system", "promoting reforming the system of classified management of the court personnel" and "promoting reforming unified management of the personnel at the lower-level courts below the provincial court" aims to scientifically standardize personnel management and justifiably allocating judicial resources, for which a number of municipalities and provinces such as Shanghai, Guangdong, Hubei have been designated as the experimental sites. A reasonable personnel assignment and scientific management cannot go without informatization; and the court personnel information management system provides complete information of each judge, while associating it to related cases. All this is conducive to integrating internal management and implementing judicial responsibility.

"Straightening up the management relations of judicial administrative affairs of courts" requires scientifically establishing the judicial administrative management platform at the people's courts, standardizing and unifying management responsibilities, and reducing as much as possible the consumption of judicial resources in administrative trivialities. "Improving in-service judge training mechanism" requires establishing an education and training net for Chinese judges, and promoting online teaching and resources sharing with the support of technology. "Improving the judge performance evaluation system" has also to be carried out on the informatization platform, which is indispensable to an effective judge performance evaluation system.

Information technology serves to boost judicial personnel management and administrative office work. Up to the end of 2015, a personnel management system had been constructed at over 90% courts across China, over 50% of the courts had constructed administrative office system and intranets. In the judicial reform experimental areas attempts began to be made to construct an information system capable of unified management of personnel and property, management of people's jurors and judge selection. The use of these judicial assistance management systems has been of great help to the management of the court personnel and the assessment of performance. The courts at Nanjing have their trial management information platform incorporating a number of modules including trial and enforcement assessment, petition assessment, and team construction assessment. With full and easy access to over 20 entries of information concerning each judge's and clerk's trial quality and efficiency, petition, innovations of performance and honesty and discipline as well, the management institutions can conduct comprehensive evaluation according to the data thereof.

In general, the *Outline of the Fourth Five-Year Reform Plan* has 35 among its 65 items of judicial reform in 7 categories directly related to or supported by the court informatization, covering the three broad areas of court practice in serving the people, serving trials and enforcement, and serving judicial management and involving 20 aspects of the court performance. Therefore promoting the court informatization will definitely support and boost judicial reform.

2.8 Concentrating big data to enhance governance

Data is a fundamental resources of a country, and is where the national competitiveness lies. The value of data is in its use, and in decision making and service management supported by big data and technology thereof. On the Fifth Plenary Session of the Eighteenth National Congress of CPC was put forward the strategy of making China a cyberpower and implementing "internet+" action plan. At the State Council Executive Meeting was approved *Platform of Action for Promoting Big Data Development*, which brought up promoting open sharing of public data resources and raising to the fundamental strategic position the application of big data.

Informatization does not only mean data production, but a good management and application of data. One of the major contents of the court informatization is the construction of a concentrated data management platform at the four-level courts, with an effectuated full coverage of the case information of all courts and the court personnel administrative management. Meanwhile, based on the concentrated data, advanced models of data analysis shall be applied of their optimal effect to the services for judicial trials, governmental decision making and socioeconomic construction. A good use of judicial big data primarily necessitates its concentration. In each link of the judicial process a large quantity of data can be produced, which used to be dispersed in the traditional judicial management mode into different levels, places and departments, hence the formation of a lot of "information isolated islands". In dealing with such data fragments the data management platform is designed to centralize data by adopting specific organization structures. And the data centralization does not simply mean physically concentrated data storage, but a process of initial data processing and analysis. And in such a process, the trial data centralization shall be carried out in terms of classified characteristics, time, and types of trial and enforcement performance at the service of deep mining and analysis of big data.

A deep mining of big data is conducive not only to enhancing judicial efficiency and judicial justice, but to the Party's decision making and social governance. Many of the judicial performance problems and difficulties of social management can be settled with a synthetic analysis on a joint action of judicial data with external data. For instance, exercising "same judgment on the homogeneous cases" as an internal requirement of judicial justice relies heavily on the data support, as provided in big data, of the trials on homogeneous cases across the country. Likewise, the difficulties of enforcement can also be effectively mitigated through synthetic analysis and use of different data resources mentioned above. Judicial trials face up to social contradictions, reflecting in part the operation condition of social management. It is thereby conducive to the study and judge the existent problems arising in social governance to timely summarize the characteristics of judicial trials and different types of cases. Moreover, an predictive analysis on economic tendency can be made by drawing on judicial big data and a diachronic analysis of trials in history with reference to social changes, thus providing quantitative data for the Party's decision making.

2.8.1 Accomplishments in concentrated management of judicial information

First of all, remarkable accomplishments have been achieved in the construction of the court trial data center pooling of massive judicial data. In June 2014, the Supreme People's Court had its data concentration management platform completed and put into operation, which was the first of its kind to converge, manage and analyze the judicial information resources from the courts across the country. The data on the platform is real-time automatically collected from the case information management systems at the courts of various levels and converged for a concentrated management without affecting the working of the client applications and increasing the judges' workloads.

A full coverage of the court data has been achieved. Up to June of 2015, the Supreme People's Court had its data concentration management platform having fully covered 3,512 courts across China. And on the platform the case data is transmitted and exchanged with the private net of courts. The Supreme People's Court has constructed the data transmission and exchange system, to which the courts at different provinces have their jurisdictions uploading and exchanging data in a gradual manner. By the end of 2015, the platform had concentrated all the case data from 3,512 courts in the country; while having established a mechanism of data transmission, updating and maintenance, 98.4% of the courts had effectuated real-time data uploading, and all the courts had effectuated daily updating of information concerning case filing, division, court sessions, process transitions and case conclusions, with an average passing rate of the data quality having reached 99.3%. Such a full coverage has been a historical breakthrough. Through the construction of four guarantee mechanisms for automatic data updating, whole process data verification, all dimension data feedback, and high standard data validation, across-database comparison had been done both manually and by computer for the finalization of the data coverage, having thus accomplished the verification of all data processing of the year 2015.

The four-level courts across China have been actively engaged in constructing the trial data center performing data concentration and sharing and conducting scientific efficient management, providing powerful data support, with its real-time dynamic data updating and open sharing mechanism, to a series of practices of trial process management, case quality inspection, trial efficacy evaluation, trial operation condition analysis, judge performance assessment and judicial openness.

Moreover, various applications have been developed on the platform, carrying out data analysis of trials and enforcement. The data management platform provides a battery of data services for the courts across the country in terms of the data condition, such as new additions, historical data, closed data and open data. And on the platform a comparative computing was conducted on 150,000 groups of tables and figures for over 19 million cases of the year. On the basis of the data management mentioned above, a directory system was also planned for judicial data resources, and accordingly a general framework of the data resources directory was teased out. Meanwhile, the platform provides the court directory service, displaying the hierarchy of all the courts across China and their related information. In addition, data analysis and special topic research were carried out on the key trials. In 2015, altogether 15 topical analyses, including those of illegal fund-raising and private lending, were completed. The data development and application has provided powerful support and technical guarantee for observations on the development tendency of court trials.

Finally, various innovations have turned up on the data concentration management at the local courts. The high court at Beijing completed its “information globe” in a three-dimensional operation mode. On the platform 1.6 million groups of data analysis figures and tables can be produced via logic computing, providing dynamic data analysis service for all the three level courts.

In 2008, the high court at Zhejiang started a project for case data concentration, setting up as of the general framework a general data center at the high court, data sub-centers at the intermediate courts, and branch data centers at the grass-roots courts, having thus formed a strategic pattern of mutual backup and individualized management, and effectuated data concentration involving the trial performance at the three level courts. Up to the later half of 2015, the data center had collected data of 10 million cases, audio and video recordings of over 2 million cases, and electronic archival documents of 1.14 billion pages in 18 million volumes, having driven the quality and efficacy of judicial management onto a new footstep.

Chongqing high court constructed a database of judicial information resources, which, by adopting cloud computing and big data technology, has turned into a cloud center of all the municipal court data with a concentration of the application system information concerning trials, administrative affairs, and teams as well as other associated data, performing deep mining and synthetic application through analysis, comparison and statistics to provide for the courts big data intelligent analysis, precise study and judgment, and dynamic monitor management. Up to August 2015, various professional resource databases had been completed in terms of archive, trials, and documents, having collected on the "cloud center" over 1.97 million cases, together with over 130,000 pieces of audio-video trial records, more than 7.25 million volumes of legal documents, and 5.46 million volumes of archives.

2.8.2 Big data in service of socioeconomic construction

Big data not only serves the internal system of courts, but more importantly, also serves socioeconomic construction through comprehensive data sharing and effective joint action with other governmental institutions and social organizations. Currently, primary success has been achieved in topic analysis on judicial data and service. The Supreme People's Court has initiated integration and mining of the trial data from the courts countrywide, providing analysis services concerning judicial statistics, trial quality and efficacy, topic analysis, and information search, while making in-depth analysis on the cases of social hot issues and of high social concerns for pre-judging signs and tendencies of potential problems.

The court informatization boosts data sharing between trial data and the data from other institutions such as police, social insurance, medicine, and education, and provides for the Party's decision making trial condition analysis reports, including case data analysis, which deals with the basic information of the defendant and ruling result, providing information support for a precise and griddized management of social security. Traditional social management adopts a griddized mode in that all the communities and streets are divided into grids. Such griddization enforces precise management, and at the same time brings forth large quantity of information concerning "personnel, localities, events, assets, and organizations". The data provided by the institutions such as police, justice, family-planning, housing management, ethnic groups and religions contribute to the formation of a three-dimensional and precise social management and bring into existence a virtual data configuration of the above-mentioned griddization management via "internet+". And in the course of making public the data of the governmental departments, the government has transformed its interrelationship with the people, who can participate via big data in the governmental decision making. Likewise, the government has its access to public opinions greatly broadened with the support of big data.

A number of high courts took initiatives in providing supporting services for the decision making at the local Party committee and government by using trial information analysis. For instance, a line management system of trials was developed for the courts at Sichuan, which, by making use of big data analysis, has been actively providing suggestions for the local Party committee and government. In recent years, deep analyses on the trial data concerning drug crime, finance, and private lending cases have been carried out successively for proposing a series of working suggestions on regulation of salient issues in social security, economic risk prevention and control, and protection of the rights and interests of the people's livelihood, which are to be submitted, in the form of written reports, to the leading figures and related institutions as well of the provincial

Party committee and government for their reference. The high court at Sichuan required that the determination of key areas for investigation and research shall be based on the big data of trials, thus to boost the quality of investigation and research. For example, it was revealed from data analysis that there had been an apparent increase in the number of retrial cases of the disputes over construction contracts in the construction engineering, and specific to which came out in 2015 *Sichuan People's High Court's Replies to Several Questions Arising in Trials on the Cases of Disputes over Construction Contracts in the Construction Engineering*, having enforced ruling standard of the homogeneous cases and therefore enhanced trial quality and efficacy. In 2014, Shandong High People's Court, in dealing with the problem of abrupt increase in the finance-involving disputes, put forward suggestions on strengthening financial regulation and standardizing financial order, and got adopted of such by Shandong provincial government.

2.9 Boosting the construction of honest and clean courts and supervising judicial power exercising

In spite of the remarkable accomplishments in honest and clean court construction, problems still exist and remain to be solved that the honest government system has not been well implemented, that supervision not properly applied, that procedures not well observed in case handling, and even that there have been violations of laws and disciplines. All these strongly necessitate constructing honest and clean courts by way of informatization.

2.9.1 An application system for discipline inspection and supervision

It has been pointed out at the Fourth Plenary Session of the Eighteenth National Congress of CPC that the power limits shall be made clear of each level administration within the judicial jurisdictions and an internal supervision and restriction mechanism shall be improved, that the personnel within the judicial institutions shall not be in violation of regulations by intervening into the case handling in someone else's charge, and that a recording system and a responsibility investigation system must be established and targeted at the judicial personnel's involvement in any case handling. It has been put forward thereby in the *Outline of the Fourth Five-Year Reform Plan* that the judicial inspection, trial supervision, and honesty inspection shall be improved and strengthened, that an investigation mechanism of discipline violations shall be established with the superior discipline inspection commission and superior courts taking the lead and the lower-level courts acting in coordination and cooperation and to effectuate an orderly connection of the discipline inspection and supervision with the disciplinary punishment of judge, that that a recording system and a responsibility investigation system shall be established and targeted at the judicial personnel's involvement in any case handling, and that regulated shall be the court personnel's contact and intercourse with the interested parties, lawyers, persons of special relationships, and intermediary organizations.

The Supreme People's Court has developed on the information platform a discipline inspection and supervision system, which performs registration, query and export to files on the instances of the leading cadres' and court personnel's taking interest in a case, having thus played an important role in anti-corruption and preventing unlawful intervention in the case handling.

2.9.2 Easy access of complaints and reporting

On the reporting online opened up at the courts countrywide, the people enjoy great convenience in performing the divine rights bestowed upon them by the Constitution. And the platform, with its advanced software and hardware technology and advantage of informatization as well as networking effect, is characterized by convenience, interactivity, supervision, high-efficiency and security, not only enabling the four-level courts across the country to form a synergy in accepting and investigating the online reporting, but also making it easier for the higher-level courts to exercise guidance and supervision on the above-mentioned tasks carried out by the lower-level courts.

The platform for reporting adopts a unified standard and consists of the front platform for uploading reporting and back platform for letter handling. The front platform is set up on the internet for collecting reporting from the people and feeding back what is going on. The people can follow the links to different reporting websites of different courts by visiting the Supreme People's Court's reporting center online (http://jubao.court.gov.cn). Whereas the back platform is set up on the private net of courts, performing analysis and handling incoming reports. Both the platforms have privacy practices to prevent any possible leakage of the reporting information and to protect the informant's rights.

The opening and linking of the reporting websites at the four-level courts across the country has been an important move to implement on the part of courts the main body responsibility in constructing the Party conduct and an honest and clean government, to further expand the passage of reporting by the people, and to thoroughly punish corruption in the realm of justice, and an effective approach as well by which the higher-level courts strengthen their supervision on the report handling at the lower-level courts. It has not only enhanced the courts' capability in discovering and investigating cases of law and discipline violations, but expanded the passage of reporting, while actively responding to the people's concerns and enabling the people to more easily perform their rights to supervise and report and therefore to feel directly judicial fairness and justice.

2.9.3 Improving the internal supervision and monitoring system

The four-level courts across the country set about strengthening the internal supervision, with the support of informatization, and exercising comprehensive, dynamic, and timely supervision on trial process, results, quality and efficiency by closely monitoring the case process as well as placing the trial and enforcement information in sunshine while enabling the people to perform external supervision to guarantee judicial justice. It can be said that through the whole-process monitoring of trials with the aid of informatization, the trial process has become open and transparent with all the tracks being recorded therein, and the whole case handling has become "visible, touchable, manageable, and accountable".

To standardize the judicial practice, a GPS system is installed on many of the court-owned vehicles to keep records of the data concerning the driving time, mileage, itinerary, and fuel consumption for preventing private use of these vehicles. And the outgoing police officers are provided with a set of "law enforcement recorder", which is used to carry out audio and video recording of the enforcement process, for the purpose of not only supervising and standardizing law enforcement, but obtaining evidence when disputes arise.

To effectively prevent and control the risk of corruption, surveillance devices are installed in office areas, corridors, courtrooms, and mediation reception rooms to conduct multiple monitoring on the interested parties' contact with the police officers, court hearings and the judge's behavior and attitude for preventing misbehavior.

2.10 Information construction in steady progress and the guarantee mechanism in constant improvement

2.10.1 Organization leadership and team construction

A team of professional personnel of informatization make up an important part of judicial assistance personnel. In June 2015, the Supreme People's Court issued *Opinions on the Team Construction of Informatization Personnel* and explicitly required that the professional personnel of informatization be included in the judicial assistance team, while having specified requirements for the office setup and professional structure configuration thereof. At each of the courts of different levels was set up a leading group for informatization. And at the Supreme People's Court was set up an information center; at various high courts were set up information technology institutions; at some intermediate and grass-roots courts were set up special institutions or employed specialists in related offices.

At present, the courts across the country have built up a team of 7,200 specialists, among them there are over 5,300 regular staff and 1,900 contract-based employees, whose professional quality is to be constantly improved through technical training, long-distance communication, topic lectures, seminars and topic investigations.

2.10.2 Maintenance guarantee and information safety

The guarantee construction of informatization of courts has been in steady progress, with the maintenance guarantee system having come into its basic formation. A major mode of operating and maintaining of infrastructure is outsourcing service. The courts of all levels invested 168 million RMB yuan in the yearly maintenance; over 1,400 technicians were engaged in the outsourcing service. A large majority of high courts have had standardized performance in the operation and maintenance and implementation of infrastructure. Such a work was extended to data and safety operation and maintenance. About 50% high courts implemented data operation and maintenance by way of self-service or outsourcing service, while a small number of courts at Beijing adopted outsourcing service. In the process visualized operation and maintenance has become an effective means to manage and control the operation of information system, which has been adopted by 50% high courts to conduct dynamic monitoring on various facilities, so as to find out and handle problems before hand for guaranteeing stable operation of information system.

Also in steady advancement has been the hierarchical protection of information system. According to statistics, 78% of the courts have implemented hierarchical protection; 28% have carried out rectification and assessment on the important information system on the private net; 16% have done the work on the important information system on internet; 19% have done the work on the important information system on the external private net.

3. The direction of future work

The Strategic Plan for State Informatization Development (2006-2020), issued by General Office of the CPC Central Committee and General Office of the State Council, states that since informatization is a world tendency and an impetus for socioeconomic reforms, promoting informatization in all aspects is not only a strategic initiative of the overall modernization construction, but also a demand of implementing the Scientific Outlook on Development, and building China into a comprehensive well-off, harmonious and innovation-oriented society. *The Thirteenth Five-year Plan for National Economic and Social Development (2016-2020)* points out that China will further deepen the reform of judicial system to respect judicial rules, promote judicial fairness, improve legal guarantee and supervision of rights, and calls for a harmonious development of economy and society through boosting the synchronous development of new-type industrialization, informatization, urbanization and agricultural modernization, thus strengthening our nation's hard power and soft power as well. In the context of comprehensively advancing rule of law, the mounting challenges of realizing people-oriented court informatization and the arduous mission of meeting people's judicial needs offer a golden opportunity for the scientific development of judicial system. In 2015, the Supreme People's Court began to upgrade the court information system to version 3.0, and employ new technology to transform the court into a customer-oriented one to serve the people, trial and enforcement and judicial administration, with *Reform Outline* and *A Five-Year Development Plan for the Information Construction of the People's Courts (2016-2020)* as the guidance, accelerating the modernization of trial system and trial capability as the goal, thereby promoting the transformation and upgrading of court information construction, which will provide a solid technological guarantee of its scientific development.

The construction of version 3.0 aims at facilitating the modernization of trial system and trial capability and building a "smart court" that will deal with lawsuits online, open enforcement of judgments, provide all-round and integrated information resource service and assistant decision support.

A Five-Year Development Plan for the Informatization of the People's Courts (2016-2020) outlines the following six features of version 3.0.

1) Full coverage. People's courts at all levels are to improve the overall planning and top-level design with the guidance of "Tianping Project", employ such new technologies as network and cloud computation to realize a full coverage of four-level court networks, including judicial trial, personnel, administrative affairs and lawsuit procedures; and realize a full coverage of fixed and mobile networks, including judicial information resources and diversified judicial needs of litigants, the public and pertinent government departments. And the ultimate goal is to form an interconnected, unimpeded and

resource-sharing informationalized court network.

2) Mobile interconnection. People's courts at all levels are to explore mobile business with the aid of network and mobile applications. Public-oriented mobile applications are expected to be developed to provide real-time litigation service and judicial transparency for clients, solicitors and the public, and, on the other hand, to enhance judges' efficiency in case handling. Development of applications in regard to circuit trial, enforcement, delivery and VPN service of people's court is to be boosted and the mobile terminal application of virtual office be steadily advanced.

3) Cross-sectorial integration. People's courts at all levels are to integrate and expand various infrastructures, application systems and info-resources employing such technologies as cloud computing, data sharing and exchanging, thereby realizing the interconnection of all institutions, access to external networks of pertinent departments, integration of terminal treatment and frontal management. In this way, informatization can best serve the people, enforcement of judgments and judicial management.

4) In-depth application. People's courts at all levels are to make the best of abundant case resources and improve the application of big data and cloud computation. They are also expected to expand case study, analyze and grasp the developing trend, characteristics and rules of the enforcement of judgments under new circumstances based on data-driven concept, thus providing information and decision-making services for court construction, state and society governance.

5) Transparency and convenience. People's courts at all levels are to upgrade judicial credibility and further achieve judicial transparency by making public on the three platforms judicial information of each court. In addition, people's courts at all levels are to provide the litigant with variable, convenient, customer-friendly online and offline litigation services.

6) Safety and controllability. People's courts at all levels are to improve risk management capacity of basic information networks and important information systems through raising information security awareness, improving information assurance mechanism, building a definite network accountability system, enhancing safeguard level of basic information networks and important information systems and practicing the requirements of hierarchical protection with the aid of advanced information security technology, thereby ensuring information security in the process of informatization.

At present, the Supreme People's Court demands to build "smart courts", which can regulate judicial acts by recording all traces of a trial utilizing information technology and ultimately establish a comprehensive, mobile, interconnected, transparent, convenient, and safe intelligent information system by the end of 2017. Another requirement of the Supreme People's Court is perfecting the three judicial information platforms and data integrated management platform to reinforce big data analysis and unify judgment standards, thus improving ruling standardization. Thirdly, the court ought to offer judicial suggestions specific to the problems arising in trial data, and to enhance social governance. In addition, the court is required to carry forward the construction of digital archives and realize electronic servicing of case files. Yet problems still exist in the informatization process such as there being outdated concepts, unbalanced development, failure of implementation of planning, inefficient application, underdeveloped management mechanism and unqualified personnel. The following efforts are expected to be devoted to satisfying the requirements of informatization version 3.0.

3.1 Upgrading conception and revolutionizing the judicial system with informatization

The top priority of court informatization should be given to helping the court staff change ideas and fully recognize the significance of informatization. While people's courts at all levels have taken the task seriously under the requirement of the Supreme People's Court, the following misunderstandings still exist. It is common that some staff take it as the job of information technology sectors or administrative departments, thus showing an indifferent and negative attitude. It is regarded as a pain in the neck for some judges and some other relevant staff who are not familiar with information technology on account of possible extra work. The ambivalent attitudes above resulted in such problems as inefficiency of online case handling, low coverage rate and lagging uploading of written judgments.

Informatization will have a profound influence on the court reform. The court is going to undergo a revolution, since the court informatization will greatly change its traditional work patterns, means of communication with other sectors and reclusive image, which is absolutely a restriction to enforcement of judgments. In the information age, the judicial agency is obliged to follow the trend and move forward through utilizing information technology. Informatization may not seem a kernel work itself of courts, yet it is a powerful instrument to enhance the kernel work effectively. The trial data processing, which used to be sample-based local and incomplete analysis, has turned into comprehensive analysis based on full-scale collection of data, thus greatly improving judgment accuracy. It is certain that the court informatization will result in open and transparent judicial information, interlocked processes of trial and enforcement, clean and devoted judges with qualified professional ability.

It is required that people's courts at all levels be fully aware of the significance of the court informatization and integrate it into all court routines so as to serve the enforcement of judgments, serve the people and court management. Under new circumstances with social interest differentiation and emerging contradictions, the court is obliged, by means of informatization, to upgrade judicial credibility, maintain its authority and safeguard the people's interests, and successfully carry out its mission.

3.2 Making top-level design for an overall coordinated advancement of the court information system

There is no doubt that all the routine court work has enjoyed the benefits of informatization construction with its rapid development and innovations. Yet, we also have to recognize the national situation that informatization infrastructure, technical personnel, funds and equipment demanded in the process vary from one court to another due to the fact that China is a developing country with vast territory. Therefore, it is crucial to perfect the top-level design, move forward the informatization project systematically and step by step according to the various local situations, so as to reduce costs to a minimum. However, the following current problems do exist: the incomprehensive top-level design results in its ineffective guidance; information resources can not be effectively shared due to redundant platforms, lack of a unified and accepted standard, and incompatibility of software systems; there lacks of a quality evaluation index system, targeted core technologies and pre-studies on them; a comprehensive management operating mechanism has not come into existence; there is no legal support for such applications as electronic delivery service; its private network does not cover all courts and the bandwidth of some courts are inadequate to a varying extent; data computing and storage equipment of data management platform can not satisfy the increasing demands of routine work, hence the sharing difficulty of audio and video system; it's still impossible to communicate with relevant institutions via the private network; business collaboration is not realized on a large scale due to the low efficiency of cross-network information exchange; on account of the dispersed channel, narrow coverage and inadequate popularization and application of achievements, it used to be a common practice that more efforts were attached to construction itself instead of application; effective mechanisms of achievement evaluation, notification and improvement have not been built yet mainly because of the absence of the ideas and methods of achievement evaluation.

In order to encourage information publicity nationwide, the Supreme People's Court has constructed a great number of websites for opening specialized information, and many a local court built their own (see Table 1). Take the network of government affairs for instance, quite a few courts set up websites of judicial publicity and litigation service portal as well, the functions of which overlap; in addition, some courts even construct a judicial publicity website besides the government website. Ever since 2014, online litigation platforms and websites for judicial service have been constructed one after another, some of which are on commercial websites, making it rather difficult for the public to decide whether they are the courts' official information. Furthermore, due to their overlapped functions, the same piece of information has to be uploaded to different websites, which not only increases the cost, but creates more trouble for the public to search for information. In addition, docking of state websites with local ones has not reached the desired effect which demands an integration of those platforms.

Table 1 A list of court websites

Object	Government Gateway Websites	The Portal for Local Courts on China Court Net	Judicial Openness Websites	Litigation Service Websites	Local Websites on private net
The Supreme People's Court	www.court.gov.cn		www.court.gov.cn/zgsplcxxgkw		111.205.123.169:8080/ssfww
Beijing High People's Court	www.bjcourt.gov.cn	Bjgy.chinacourt.org/index.shtml	www.bjcourt.gov.cn	www.bjcourt.gov.cn	bjfyzb.chinacourt.org
Tianjin High People's Court		fjfy.chinacourt.org			
Hebei Provincial High People's Court	www.hebeicourt.gov.cn	hbfy.chinacourt.org	hbgy.hbsfgk.org	hbgy.hbsfgk.org	hbdzfy.gov.cn http://121.28.48.74
Shanxi Provincial High People's Court		shanxify.chinacourt.org/index.shtml		gy.shanxify.gov.cn	
High People's Court of The Inner Mongolia Autonomous Region		nmgf.chinacourt.org/index.shtml	nmgy.susong51.com	nmgy.susong51.com	
Liaoning Provincial High People's Court		lnfy.chinacourt.org	www.lnsfy.gov.cn		
Jilin Provincial High People's Court	courts.jl.gov.cn/jgsz/jlgy	jlfy.chinacourt.org	www.jlsfy.gov.cn		www.e-court.gov.cn
Heilongjiang Provincial High People's Court	www.hljcourt.gov.cn		www.hljcourt.gov.cn/sfgk	Hljgy.susong51.com	tv.hljcourt.gov.cn
Shanghai High People's Court	www.hshfy.sh.cn/shfy/gweb/index.html	shfy.chinacourt.org/index.shtml	www.hshfy.sh.cn/shfy/gweb/index_dh.jsp		
Jiangsu Provincial High People's Court	www.jsfy.gov.cn		221.226.175.76:8038/webapp/area/jsgy/wsgk/wsgk.jsp	ssfw.jsfy.gov.cn	
Zhejiang Provincial High People's Court	www.zjcourt.cn		www.zjsfgkw.cn		www.zjcourt.cn www.zjwsf.gov.cn lsfpt.zjsfgkw.cn

(Contd.)

Object	Government Gateway Websites	The Portal for Local Courts on China Court Net	Judicial Openness Websites	Litigation Service Websites	Local Websites on private net
Anhui Provincial High People's Court	www.ahcourt.gov.cn		www.ahgyss.cn	www.ahgyss.cn	www.ahcourt.gov.cn:7000
Fujian Provincial High People's Court	www.fjcourt.gov.cn	fjfy.chinacourt.org/index.shtml	www.fjcourt.gov.cn	http://ssfw.fjcourt.gov.cn	www.fjcourt.gov.cn/page/court/Tszb
Jiangxi Provincial High People's Court		jxfy.chinacourt.org	www.jxfy.gov.cn/web/root/index.jsp#news		
Shandong Provincial High People's Court	www.sdcourt.gov.cn/sdfy/349727/index.html	Sdfy.chinacourt.org/index.shtml	www.sdcourt.gov.cn		123.233.248.122
Henan Provincial High People's Court	www.hncourt.gov.cn	hnfy.chinacourt.org/	ssfw.hncourt.gov.cn/	ssfw.hncourt.gov.cn/	ts.hncourt.gov.cn/
Hubei Provincial High People's Court	www.hbfy.gov.cn	hubeigy.chinacort.org			
Hunan Provincial High People's Court		hunanfy.chinacourt.org/			
Guangdong Provincial High People's Court	www.gdcourts.gov.cn		http://www.gdcourts.gov.cn/gdgy/s		gd.xinshiyun.com
High People's Court of Guangxi Zhuang Autonomous Region	www.gxcourt.gov.cn	gxfy.chinacourt.org	yggx.gxcourt.gov.cn		171.106.48.55:18898
Hainan Provincial High People's Court	www.hicourt.gov.cn		http://ssfw.hicourt.gov.cn	http://ssfw.hicourt.gov.cn	
Chongqing High People's Court		cqfy.chinacourt.org/index.shtml	www.cqfygzfw.gov.cn	www.cqfygzfw.gov.cn	
Sichuan Provincial High People's Court	www.sccourt.gov.cn		sfgk.sccourt.gov.cn		zxgk.sccourt.gov.cn

(Contd.)

Object	Government Gateway Websites	The Portal for Local Courts on China Court Net	Judicial Openness Websites	Litigation Service Websites	Local Websites on private net
Guizhou Provincial High People's Court	www.guizhoucourt.cn		http://www.guizhoucourt.cn/splcgk/index.jhtml	http://www.guizhoucourt.cn/gzfwpt/index.jhtml#	http://58.16.65.95:8080/rdapp/pcuser/rd/login.do http://lxxt.guizhoucourt.cn/loginAction/pheneInit.htm/login_role=5&fy=3250
Yunnan Provincial High People's Court	www.gy.yn.gov.cn		www.ynfy.gov.cn	yngy.ynfy.gov.cn	
High People's Court of Tibet Autonomous Region			Xzgy.susong51.com		
Shanxi Provincial High People's Court		sxfy.chinacourt.org	www.sxgaofa.cn	www.sxgaofa.cn	www.sxgaofa.cn/ts/today
Gansu Provincial High People's Court	www.chinagscourt.gov.cn		gsgf.gssfgk.com		61.178.55.5:8081/ssxf/index.jsp
High People's Court of Ningxia Hui Autonomous Region	www.nxfy.gov.cn				
Qinghai Provincial High People's Court		qhfy.chinacourt.org	www.qhcourt.gov.cn		
High People's Court of Xinjiang Uygur Autonomous Region	www.xjcourt.org				
Datong Intermediate People's Court		dtzy.chinacourt.org/index.shtml	dtzy.shanxify.gov.cn		
Dalian Intermediate People's Court		www.court.dl.gov.cn			

(Contd.)

Object	Government Gateway Websites	The Portal for Local Courts on China Court Net	Judicial Openness Websites	Litigation Service Websites	Local Websites on private net
Guangzhou Intermediate People's Court	www.gzcourt.org.cn				
Taiyuan Intermediate People's Court		tyzy.chinacourt.org/	tyzy.shanxify.gov.cn		
Wuxi Intermediate People's Court		wxzy.chinacourt.org			
Changsha Intermediate People's Court		cszy.chinacourt.org			
Changchun Intermediate People's Court	cczy.chinacourt.org	courts.jl.gov.cn/jgsz/cczy	cczy.jlsfy.gov.cn		
Lanzhou Intermediate People's Court	www.chinagscourt.gov.cn/zy.htm/site=lanzhou		www.lzxourt.org:8090	lzcourt.org:8091/lzssfy	lzcourt.org:8092/lztszb
Ningbo Intermediate People's Court	www.nbcourt.gov.cn				
Benxi Intermediate People's Court	bxzy.chinacourt.org/index.shtml		bxzy.lnsfy.gov.cn		221.203.113.182/netvod/vodindex/index.html
Shijiazhuang Intermediate People's Court	sjzzy.hebeicourt.gov.cn		sjzzy.hbsfgk.org		www.sfyzx.com
Hefei Intermediate People's Court	court.hefei.gov.cn				
Jilin Intermediate People's Court		jlzy.chinacourt.org	jlzy.jlsfy.gov.cn		
Chengdu Intermediate People's Court		cdfy.chinacourt.org	sfgk.cdfy12368.gov.cn:153		118.114.244.67:150/index

(Contd.)

Object	Government Gateway Websites	The Portal for Local Courts on China Court Net	Judicial Openness Websites	Litigation Service Websites	Local Websites on private net
Shantou Intermediate People's Court	www. stcourts.gov. cn				
Xining Intermediate People's Court		xnzy.chinacourt. org			
Xi'an Intermediate People's Court	xazyold. china.court. org	xazy.chinacourt. org			
Qiqihar Intermediate People's Court	qqherzy. hljcourt.gov. cn		Qqhezy. susong51.com		
Fushun Intermediate People's Court		fszy.chinacourt. org	fszy.lnsfy.gov. cn		
Shenyang Intermediate People's Court		syzy.chinacourt. org	syzy.lnsfy. gov.cn		
Suzhou Intermediate People's Court	www. szzjrmfy.gov. cn		61.155.211. 18/szssfw		
Handan Intermediate People's Court	www.hdzy. gov.cn		hdzy.hbsfgk. org		
Kunming Intermediate People's Court	kmzy.ynfy. gov.cn	kmzy.chinacourt. org			
Hangzhou Intermediate People's Court	www. hzcourt.cn				
Zhengzhou Intermediate People's Court	zzfy.hncourt. gov.cn				
Wuhan Intermediate People's Court	www.whzy. hbfy.gov.cn		www. wuhancourt. gov.cn/ webapp/area/ wh/index.jsp		

(Contd.)

Object	Government Gateway Websites	The Portal for Local Courts on China Court Net	Judicial Openness Websites	Litigation Service Websites	Local Websites on private net
Qingdao Intermediate People's Court	qdzy.sdcourt. gov.cn				
Nanjing Intermediate People's Court	www. njfy,gov.cn			221.231. 143.7/ssfwzx/ webapp/ area/ nj/i ndex.jsp	nj.sifayun.com
Nanchang Intermediate People's Court		Nczy.chinacourt. org/index.shtml			
Harbin Intermediate People's Court	hebzy. hljcourt.gov. cn		Hrbzy. susong51.com		
Luoyang Intermediate People's Court	hnlyzy. hncourt.gov. cn		Lyfy. susong51.com		
Jinan Intermediate People's Court	www.jnfyw. gov.cn/ jnzyinfoplat	jinanzy. sdcourt.gov.cn/ jinnazy/376200/ index.html	jinanzy. sdcourt. gov. cn/jinnazy/ 376241/index. html		www.jnfyw.gov. cn/jnzyinfoplat/ platformData/ infoplat/pub/ infy_2632/include_ page/wsfy.jsp
Guiyang Intermediate People's Court	www. gycourt.gov. cn	gyzy. guizhoucourt.cn	gyzy. guizhoucourt. cn/sfgk/inedx. jhtml	gyzy. guizhoucourt. cn/gzfwpt/ index.jhtml	
Tangshan Intermediate People's Court	tszy. hebeicourt. gov.cn		tszy.hbsfgk. org		
Xuzhou Intermediate People's Court	xzzy. chinacourt. org	xzzy.chinacourt. org/old/fyjj	221.229. 255.26:8080/ ssfwzx		
Haikou Intermediate People's Court	www.hkfy. gov.cn				
Zhuhai Intermediate People's Court	www. zhcourt.gov. cn				www.hizh.cn/court

(Contd.)

Object	Government Gateway Websites	The Portal for Local Courts on China Court Net	Judicial Openness Websites	Litigation Service Websites	Local Websites on private net
Zibo Intermediate People's Court	zbzy.sdcourt.gov.cn				
Huainan Intermediate People's Court		hnzy.chinacourt.org			
Shenzhen Intermediate People's Court	www.szcourt.gov.cn		ssfw.szcourt.gov.cn		
Xiamen Intermediate People's Court	www.xmcourt.gov.cn				
Fuzhou Intermediate People's Court		fzszy.chinacourt.org			
Anshan Intermediate People's Court		aszy.chinacourt.org			
Urumqi Intermediate People's Court	www.urumqicourt.org		221.181.38.141:8003/wlmqssfwzz		
Nanning Intermediate People's Court	nnzy.chinacourt.org/index.shtml	nnzy.gxcourt.gov.cn/index.htm	ygnn.gxcourt.gov.cn		
Yinchuan Intermediate People's Court	yczy.nxfy.gov.cn				
Hohhot Intermediate People's Court		Hhhtzy.chinacourt.org/index.shtml			
Lhasa Intermediate People's Court			Xzgy.susong51.net		
Baotou Intermediate People's Court		btzy.chinacourt.org/index.shtml	btfy.susong51.com		

To solve the universal problem of weak overall planning and top-level design in the court informatization process, the Supreme People's court and local courts at all levels are required to further improve the top-level design regarding development planning, global technical scheme, technical standard, evaluation index system, management mechanism and technological innovation, thereby providing scientific guidance for the court informatization project. As for local courts at all levels, a feasible information system should be built based on the top-level design and local specific circumstances so as to prevent redundancy and waste of resources. At the same time, the top-level design is strongly advised to be made based on a thorough research and the practical situation of China.

3.3 Mastering judicial regularities for an in-depth coalescence of IT and court operations

A threshold of the project is to realize the system development by coordinating the new one with the old one. It's a fact that quite a number of platforms have been set up by people's courts at all levels, and that many systems and software have been developed. However, we must not ignore another fact, that is, they can not satisfy the increasing demands of court operation. The following problems are salient in particular: many application systems provide a variety of functions which are not compatible with each other; the court private network cannot dock with external service applications effectively; there is no unified portal to litigation and service integration; the case information management system doesn not meet the standards of trial and enforcement laid down in *Reform Outline*; support for the coordination between the superior and lower-level courts, courts of different regions, courts and relevant judicial institutions is insufficient; the network-aided trial system can not effectively fulfill the task of facilitating case handling; such capabilities as mobile officing and case handling, exchange of e-files and file management should be improved urgently; the traditional personnel management system can not meet judicial reform's requirements of centralized management of human, financial and material resources and dynamic regulation of judges; the development of administrative affairs management system is uneven; litigation service platform can not provide a kind of "one-stop" service for various parties involved; the application system of judgments needs to move forward from being available to easy-to-use and useful; some application system even increased judges' burden to an extent, to name just a few.

It is emphasized by General Secretary Xi Jinping that "judicial act has its unique property and rule, and judicial power is the power to judge the facts of cases and the law. " Therefore, to ascertain the truth and apply the law appropriately are the permanent pursuit of judicial judgment. Whereas, the essence of informatization calls for utilizing information technology to make judicial operation more scientific and reasonable, prevent and decrease the uncertainty, reduce operation costs, maximize benefits while minimizing loss, which are in accordance with judicial operation rules. Therefore, it is strongly advised to take the rules and mission of judicial act into consideration while developing systems and software.

As for grasping judicial rules, the following suggestions are put forward. Firstly, resorting to information technology, the procedure of trial and enforcement is to be reconstructed, by which all traces of trial are to be recorded and real time superintendence is to be effected. Secondly, relying on information management system, the trial mode is to be reformed and instant communication between police officers and chief justices is to be realized so as to achieve institutionalized, legalized and flat-style administration and enhance judicial management efficiency. Thirdly, every link, node, position and staff involved in enforcement of judgments are to be more strictly supervised through a dynamic monitor. Moreover, justice policies and measurements are to be adjusted and optimized based on the public's demands, changes of each variety of cases and scientific analysis of trial development captured via the information centralized platform, thereby enhancing the timeliness and pertinence of decision-making. In addition, personnel management efficiency is to be enhanced through the statistical analysis of personnel information in information management system, in which it is possible for administrators and decision-makers to keep up with police officer's information in a digital and visual way, and a judge can have a clear picture of his case handling in real time to promote judges' self-discipline, self-evaluation and self-management. At last, informatization is to be fully integrated into court affairs through developing an information-aided system, broadening information infrastructure and integrating business application system, information resource management system and service system for the trial and trial administration.

3.4 Balancing supply and demand and assisting in trial enforcement in service of the people

The value of the court informatization program lies in facilitating judicial trials to function well and satisfying judicial demands of the public, which is the ultimate goal as well. However, there is a gap between supply of information and its increasing demand. On the one hand, judicial staff are in urgent need of informatization to improve work efficiency and quality due to their heavy workload of case handling; on the other hand, the present informatization program can not meet the real need in that there are such problems as lack of unified data standard, sharing difficulty, heavy workload of manual input, inaccurate data, incomplete node and low level of user-friendly interface. Therefore, the development of court informatization both in scope and in depth requires its organic integration of judicial adjudication and management so as to reduce redundant information, optimize case-handling process and enhance work efficiency.

The court informatization ought to provide client, attorney and the public with convenient, efficient and real time service. However, at present, the scattered and overlapping platforms is likely to be of inconvenience for information inquiry; the varied levels of website construction (with the aim to open information and provide convenience for the public) may have an impact on the efficiency of informatization.

Resorting to technical means, we conducted a survey on the government websites of 31 high people's courts, 412 intermediate people's courts and 3,168 basic people's courts through out the country. In practice, only 2,040 websites, including those of 49 high people's courts, 355 intermediate people's courts, 2,037 basic people's courts, were monitored (it is worth noting that some websites were not monitored because domain names of 69 websites could not be found and most websites with "chinacourt" in the domain name did not allow to be monitored; besides, two websites of some courts, if any, were both monitored.). The following table clearly demonstrates monitoring indexes of the survey, including unavailabe, updating columns on home page, those being indexed by search engines, invalid links, attachments not able to be downloaded, and obvious wrongly-written or mis-pronounced characters (for such specific information as its definition, monitoring period and frequency, please refer to Table 2).

Table 2 Monitoring indexes

Index	Definition	Period	Frequency
unavailability	To count the percentage of homepage unavailability within 15 seconds	a week	once every 5 minutes
updating of columns on home page	To check if the home page has been updated in the last 2 weeks	a week	once per day
being indexed by search engines	To check if the home page can be found by such search engines as Baidu and Sogou	a week	once per day
invalid links on home page	To count the number of invalid links on home page	a week	once per day
invalid links on pages except home page	To count the number of invalid links on pages except home page	a week	once per day
attachments not able to be downloaded	To count the number of attachments that cannot be downloaded or opened	a week	once per day
obviously wrongly-written or mis-pronounced characters	To count the number of wrongly-written or mis-pronounced characters that caught the media's attention or may have adverse impacts. For instance: wrongly written name of our country, state institutions, state and CPC leaders; error messages that are contrary to socialist core values.	a week	once per day
contents able to be copied or not	To check if the contents of website can be copied and pasted	a week	once per day

Results of the survey:

1) Unavailability. In the 49 home pages of high people's courts surveyed, 28.57% could not be retrieved, while home pages with less than 1% unavailability rate account for 36.73% and the rest 34.69% are home pages with greater than or equal to 1%. For the 492 home pages of intermediate people's courts, the percentages of three types mentioned above are 29.07%, 31.91%, 39.02% respectively. As for the 2040 home pages of basic people's courts, 28.48%, 32.21% and 39.31% respectively.

2) Updating of columns on home page. 81.63% of high people's courts home pages, 71.14% of intermediate people's courts home pages and 22.65% of basic people's courts home pages have updated contents, which shows high people's courts and intermediate people's courts have done a better job in this respect.

3) Being indexed by search engines. 48 home pages of high people's courts, 483 home pages of intermediate people's courts and 799 home pages of basic people's courts could be found by search engines, which account for 97.96%, 98.17% and 39.17% in their category respectively. The statistics above show that basic people's courts need to improve their home pages in search engine index.

4) Invalid links on home page. 24 home pages of high people's courts, 255 home pages of intermediate people's courts and 1,095 home pages of basic people's courts do not have this problem, which account for 48.98%, 51.83% and 53.68% in their category respectively. There were less than 10 invalid links on 40.82% home pages of high people's courts, 42.07% home pages of intermediate people's courts and 44.26% home pages of basic people's courts. As for the home pages with more than 10 invalid links, the percentages are 10.20%, 5.89%, 2.01% respectively, with one intermediate people's court home page and 1 intermediate people's court home page being inaccessible.

5) Invalid links on pages except home page. 20 websites of high people's courts, 255 websites of intermediate people's courts and 1,095 websites of basic people's courts do not have this problem, which account for 40.82%, 43.90% and 50.83% in their category respectively. There were less than 10 invalid links on 36.73% websites of high people's courts, 36.99% websites of intermediate people's courts and 39.17% that of basic people's courts. As for pages other than home page with more than 10 invalid links, the percentages are 22.45%, 18.90%, 9.95% respectively, with one intermediate people's court website and one grass-roots people's court website inaccessible.

6) Attachments not able to be downloaded. Attachments were able to be downloaded on 41 websites of high people's courts, 468 websites of intermediate people's courts and 1,990 websites of basic people's courts, which account for 83.67%, 95.12% and 97.55% in their category respectively.

7) Obviously wrongly-written or mis-pronounced characters. 40 websites of high people's courts, 438 websites of intermediate people's courts and 1,933 websites of grass-roots people's courts do not have this problem, which account for 81.63%, 89.02% and 94.75% in their category respectively.

8) Contents able to be copied or not. There was no restriction on copying contents on all the websites of high people's courts, 99.39% websites of intermediate people's courts

and 99.61% websites of grass-roots people's courts.

From the statistics above, it's obvious that government websites of local courts performs well in general, nevertheless, such problems as fluctuation of service and invalid links cannot meet the needs of the public.

Therefore, the development of court informatization is to be demand-driven so as to better serve the enforcement of judgments, judicial administration and the public. To promote the modernization of trial system and trial capability utilizing information, the following three proposals are put forward.

1) To serve the enforcement of judgments. Informatization is to become a vital carrier of online working, registering, case handling, inquiry and appealing resorting to information network system and litigation platforms, which will facilitate judges' case handling. Information construction with respect to trial, enforcement, appeal and petition, trial administration and support ought to provide judges and police officers with "convenient, coordinated and smart" enforcement of judgments applications so as to enhance trial efficiency and guarantee fair justice.

2) To serve the judicial administration. With such concepts as "big data, large scale, great service" as guidance, informatization is to be applied to fields of administrative affairs, archives management, personnel management, discipline inspection and supervision, financial administration and logistic equipment management, so as to provide leaders of all levels and administrative institutions with management means aided by "concentrated data, visible process and meticulous management", thereby improving judicial decision-making and scientific management.

3) To serve the public. In the process of court informatization, the judicial demands of the public are to be better satisfied and it is to be more convenient for parties concerned to participate in a lawsuit, thereby safeguarding fairness and justice among the public. Driven by the requirements of the plan: "internet +" to benefit the people, the courts at all levels are to provide the public with judicial services of "regular judicial publicity, incorporate litigation and varied legal propaganda", through platforms of judicial publicity, litigation service, legal propaganda, supervision and recommendation. Based on the three platforms of judicial publicity and the new media, a fast and convenient communication channel is to be built, which will provide only the true and symmetrical information and guarantee the timely interaction between the court and parties concerned in a lawsuit, so as to balance the aggregate demands of the public and aggregate judicial supply, and guarantee the public's rights to know, participate, voice and supervise, thereby realizing both the legislative and social effect of case handling.

3.5 Improving data analysis and serviceability for a better service to socioeconomic development

The utilization of big data is conducive to building a modern governance system and enhancing state governance. Nevertheless, in real practice, people's courts at all levels show insufficient management abilities of the data-concentrated management platforms, thus operating with varied data-concentrated scope and low-quality data, which is proved by courts' disclosed information. For one thing, the disclosed information is not updated in time. Take the litigation guide for example, it ought to be updated in line with the amendment of legislative documents. However, quite a number of them surveyed were still using regulations of expired laws. As for the 31 high people's courts and 49 intermediate people's courts surveyed, 61.25% of them failed to update the information concerning administrative proceedings in litigation guide. In addition, not all the information input is accurate. Take the information of case nodes for instance, which were input manually before informatization, thus leading to wrong or inaccurate information.

A system of sharing and exchanging data between higher and lower courts, courts and other departments, different networks was under-constructed, causing the isolation of information. The integration level of data resources and service capability are to be improved to offer fully covered, high-quality smart analysis for the public's participation in litigation, legal propaganda, efficient allocation of judicial resources, serving social governance and public decision-making. A standardized system of data management has not come into being, and the mechanism regarding data development, service and security is in urgent need of improvement. In a word, "big data, cloud technology" has not been essentially applied into the court services.

In the context of "big data era", the work of courts will not satisfy the demand of socioeconomic development unless they follow the trend to share information and platforms with other institutions.

To achieve the objective of enhancing judicial credibility and maintaining judicial authority by providing better services for the people, enforcement of judgments, and judicial administration, the data resources collected in judicial judgment and management process are to be developed and utilized rationally. In judicial management, big data can be applied in forming a flat-style management mode and reconstructing trial structure, so as to enhance the courts' work efficiency. As for judicial judgment, the exploitation of big data can help the party and government offices discover the present social contradictions in summarizing the characteristics, rule and running state of judicial activities in history, thus providing data basis for policy-making. In addition, the relationship between caseload, types of contradiction and social-economic development can be discovered through analyzing the big data of judiciary and socioeconomic development with certain mathematical model. In general, as one barometer of socioeconomic the big data of judiciary can be used to serve the social-economic development.

Therefore, it is required that people's courts at all levels enhance the abilities of generating and collecting information regarding enforcement of judgments and security management, improve the accuracy and standardization of data, and collaboratively develop data mining, analytical methods and output effect with information specialists of other institutions.

3.6 Strengthening team construction for training and exchange of excellent specialists in the court information

The present team of information personnel can not satisfy the demands of judicial work in the new era due to lack of specialized talents. The information system and software are not compatible with judicial work in practice in that there is a gap between demands and system development due to the fact that the information personnel are not familiar with judicial work. It is likely that the desired effects are not attained because of asynchronized data from trial and administration, thus hindering the development of informatization.

The following proposals are put forward to enhance the construction of information personnel team and get the most from court informatization.

1) Perfecting the safeguard mechanism of informatization organization. Given the significance of leadership mechanism, it is required that the informatization leading groups of people's courts at all levels take the responsibility of making the overall plan, coordinating the work and leading to form a hierarchical system in which every department has a a clear division of work and performs its respective duties in the charge of corresponding leaders, thereby guaranteeing that the project will achieve its desired results.

2) Building a talent team with specialized management and information technology. It is required that people's courts at all levels be equipped with all varieties of qualified information specialists, perfect their promotion system, provide more opportunities of practice and training, thus forming a positive talent-developing mechanism.

3) Building a talent team familiar with both information technology and judicial affairs to ensure the system work well. The following three ways are advised to optimize the talent structure: selecting excellent staff with certain legal knowledge and familiar with judicial process and information technology from judicial departments, enrolling outstanding specialists from research institutes and corporations, promoting the communication between information personnel and judicial institutions to keep them up with judicial affairs and real demands of judicial departments.

4) Strengthening the training of information technology. Since whether the informatization project can keep abreast with the times is the key to the development level of court informatization, people's courts at all levels are required to strengthen the training of information technology and equip information specialists with cutting-edge ideas and knowledge.

5) Building an expert consulting system. It is advised to turn to experts in other domains for specialized support so as to facilitate the development of court informatization.

Concluding remarks

Informatization of courts is a systematic project in regard to enforcement of judgments, judicial personnel and judicial administration. The judicial reform and information construction are as important to the development of judicial cause as the wheels to a vehicle and wings to a bird. Therefore, promoting the informatization of courts is not only a significant component of deepening judicial reform, but also a powerful engine and impetus as well. The Supreme People's Court has attached great importance to its fundamental, overall and strategic role in enhancing judicial capacity, optimizing judicial system, modernizing trial system and trial capacity, better servicing the people and realizing the ultimate objective of "people-oriented administration of justice".

The results of the survey on the information construction of people's courts at all levels suggest that great improvement has been achieved in its implementation, effect and application upon years of joint efforts. In 2015, Chinese courts upgraded the information system to version 2.0 with interconnection and interoperability as main features, and the information network constructed by the four-tier courts of the country is playing an increasingly important role in the state governance system. The main achievements are summarized as following: the completion of its infrastructure, growing maturity of its kernel application system and omni-directional covered network; the improvement of service capability resulting from innovating a variety of convenience-for-people measures; the initial formation of a primary interactive framework of informatization and judicial affairs with regard to such mechanisms as IT courts, remote video trials and e-courts; the construction of information system in enforcement of judgments to further upgrade its judicial capacity and influence; the precise administering of trial in which judges are provided intelligent service and procedures can be optimized and restructured, thereby keeping up with the overall judicial work; the further judicial publicity and judicial reform in depth and breadth aided by information technology; the upgrading of governance capacity and perfecting of informatization guarantee system through the centralization of big data in judicial system that are updated in real time; so on and so forth.

Currently, the system of informatization of people's courts in China is still faced with some problems with respect to ideas and thinking, balanced development, plan implementation, level of application, management mechanism and quality of personnel. In the construction of Version 3.0, more efforts should be focused on the following aspects: advancing ideas and knowledge, further strengthening senses of responsibility, commitment and urgency to the effect that the informatization of courts is regarded as a self-revolution; making top-level design for an overall coordinated advancement of the court information system; mastering judicial regularities for an in-depth coalescence of IT and court operations; highlighting demand-oriented service to enhance the capacities of servicing the people and judicial administration; strengthening team construction for training and exchange of excellent specialists in the court information. With these efforts, the informatization of people's courts is to realize the ultimate goal of "full coverage, mobile interconnection, cross-sectorial integration, in-depth application, transparency and convenience, security and governability", thereby better serving the people, enforcement of judgment and judicial administration.

Appendixes 1: A list of the official documents for the informatization of the country-wide courts

Please visit for Chinese version http://www.fdi.gov.cn/1800000121_39_0_1_6.html
Retrieved from http://english.gov.cn/archive/

SN	Title of document	Document No.
1	Notice of the Supreme People's Court on Issuing The Planning of Court Information Network Construction	SPC* [1996] No. 54
2	Notice of the Supreme People's Court on Issuing The Interim Provisions on Administration of Court Information Network Construction (for Trial Implementation)	SPC [1996] No. 55
3	Notice of the Supreme People's Court on Issuing The Five-year Reform Outline of People's courts	SPC [1999] No. 28
4	Notice of the Supreme People's Court on Issuing The Administrative Provisions of Court Information Network Construction and The Planning of Court Information Network Construction	SPC [2002] No. 4
5	Notice of the Supreme People's Court on Setting up a Leading Group and an Office for Information Network Construction of The Supreme People's Court	SPC [2002] No. 244
6	Notice of the General Office of The Supreme People's Court and The Judicial Administrative Equipment Administration on Administrative Measures of the Use of Portable Computers (for Trial Implementation)	SPC-GO [2002] No. 265
7	Notice on Personnel Arrangement of the Leading Group and Office for Court Information Network Construction	SPC-A [2003] No. 128
8	Notice of the Supreme People's Court on Issuing The Technical Specification of Court Information Network Construction	SPC [2002] No. 248
9	Notice of the Supreme People's Court on Issuing Opinions of The Supreme People's Court on Deployment of Dedicated Devices at People's Courts	SPC [2002] No. 21
10	Notice of the Supreme People's Court on Issuing The Implement Plan of Court Information Network Construction	SPC [2003] No. 17
11	Notice of the Supreme People's Court on Several Issues Concerning Construction of First-level Private Network of Judicial System	SPC [2003] No. 105
12	Notice of the Supreme People's Court on Issuing Opinions of The Supreme People's Court on Administration of First-level Private Network Construction of Judicial System	SPC [2004] No. 105
13	Notice of the General Office of The Supreme People's Court on Issuing The Guidance of Court Network Security Secret System Construction	SPC-GO [2004] No. 317
14	Notice of the General Office of The Supreme People's Court on Issuing Measures for Submitting Information via the Private Network of The Supreme People's Court	SPC-GO[2004] No. 334

SN	Title of document	Document No.
15	Notice of the General Office of The Supreme People's Court on Issuing The Interim Provisions of the Security Management of Court Confidential Information System	SPC-GO[2004] No. 355
16	Notice of the Supreme People's Court on Issuing The Technical Proposal of Court Private Network Construction	SPC [2005] No. 17
17	Notice of the General Office of The Supreme People's Court on Issuing The Interim Provisions of Linking the Court Information System to Internet (for Trial Implementation)	SPC-GO[2004] No. 355
18	Notice of the Supreme People's Court on Issuing The Construction Scheme of Application System of Court First-level Private Network	SPC [2005] No. 70
19	Report of the Supreme People's Court on The Project of Court E-Government Construction	SPC [2005] No. 176
20	Notice of the Supreme People's Court on Issuing The Revised Technical Proposal of Court Information System Construction	SPC [2005] No. 79
21	Notice of the Supreme People's Court on Issuing The Second Five-year Reform Outline of People's Courts(2004-2008)	SPC [2005] No. 18
22	Notice of the Information Leading Group Personnel Arrangement of The Supreme People's Court	SPC-A [2006] No. 54
23	Notice of the Supreme People's Court on Issuing Decisions of The Supreme People's Court on Strengthening Work on Court Informatization	SPC [2007] No. 21
24	Notice of the General Office of The Supreme People's Court on Issuing Several opinions of Implementing Decisions of The Supreme People's Court Strengthening Work on Court Informatization	SPC [2007] No. 6
25	Report of the Supreme People's Court on Submitting the Application for Scale project of National Judicial Information System	SPC [2007] No. 76
26	Notice of the General Office of The Supreme People's Court on Issuing The Major Work of Information Leading Group in 2007 and The Office of Information Leading Group's Work Distribution of Implementing The Major Work of Information Leading Group in 2007	SPC-GO [2007] No. 157
27	Notice of the General Office of The Supreme People's Court on Issuing The Administrative Measures for the Operation and Maintenance of Court Information System	SPC-GO [2008] No. 11
28	Notice of the Supreme People's Court on Guiding Opinions on the Grading Work of Grading Important Non-Secrecy Court Information Protection	SPC [2008] No. 159
29	Notice of the Judicial Administrative Equipment Bureau of The Supreme People's Court on Issuing The Administrative Provisions of Domain Names of Court Private Network (for Trial Implementation)	SPC-J [2008] No. 71
30	Notice of the Supreme People's Court on Issuing The Technical Specifications of Court Information Construction	SPC [2008] No. 28

SN	Title of document	Document No.
31	Report of the General Office of The Supreme People's Court on Allowed Sharing Information of The Supreme People's Court in the Project of Political-legal Departments' Co-construction of Network Facilities and Sharing of Information Resources	SPC-GO [2008] No. 561
32	Notice of Personnel Re-arrangement of Members of The Supreme Court Information Leading Group	SPC-A [2009] No. 82
33	Notice of the Supreme People's Court on Issuing The Third Five-year Reform Outline of People's Courts (2009-2013)	SPC [2009] No. 14
34	Notice of the Supreme People's Court on Issuing Several Opinions on Further Strengthening and Regulating the Implementation Work	SPC [2009] No. 43
35	Notice of the Supreme People's Court on Issuing Several Opinions on Further Strengthening Judicial work's Function of Conveniencing People	SPC [2009] No. 6
36	Notice of the Supreme People's Court on Issuing Opinions on Further Strengthening the Work of Judicial Statistics	SPC [2009] No. 55
37	Notice of the Supreme People's Court on Issuing Opinions on Thoroughly Applying the Essence of Videophone Conference of National Political and Legal Work	SPC [2009] No. 59
38	Notice of the Supreme People's Court on Issuing The Six Provisions of Judicial Publicity and Several Provisions of Subjecting People's Courts to the News Media	SPC [2009] No. 58
39	Notice on Issuing Opinions on Several Issues Concerning Constructing and Perfecting the Implementation Linkage Mechanism	SPC [2010] No. 15
40	Notice of the Supreme People's Court and Central Committee Office of Public Security Commission on Issuing Measures for Incorporating Execution work of Provinces, Autonomous Regions and Municipalities into Target Responsibility Assessment of Public Security Maintenance	SPC [2010] No. 2
41	Notice of the General Office of The Supreme People's Court on Issuing The Administrative Measures for the Supreme People's Court's Network (for Trial Implementation), The Rules of Publishing Information on the Supreme People's Court's Network (for Trial Implementation) and the Measures for Management of Website Administrators of the Supreme People's Court's Network (for Trial Implementation)	SPC-GO [2010] No. 3
42	Notice of the Supreme People's Court on Carrying out the Work of Trials Concerning Cybercafe Copyright Infringement	SPC [2010] No. 50
43	Notice of the Supreme People's Court on Issuing Several Opinions on Strengthening and Perfecting People's Courts' Work of Inspection and Supervision	SPC [2010] No. 44
44	Notice of the General Office of The Supreme People's Court on Further Strengthening Administration of The Supreme People's Court's Network Information	SPC-GO [2010] No. 54

SN	Title of document	Document No.
45	Notice of the Supreme People's Court on Issuing Guidance of Strengthening Trial Quality of Grass-roots People's Courts	SPC [2010] No. 56
46	Notice of the Supreme People's Court on Issuing Provisions on Video-recording of Trials	SPC [2010] No. 33
47	Notice of the Supreme People's Court on Issues Concerning the First Phase of Scale Project Construction	SPC [2010] No. 36
48	Notice of the Supreme People's Court on Issuing The Technical Specification of Court Information Construction (Revised in 2009)	SPC [2010] No. 38
49	Notice of the General Office of The Supreme People's Court on Developing the Information Sharing and Exchanging System of First-grade Cases	SPC-GO [2010] No. 593
50	Notice of the Supreme People's Court on Issuing Several Opinions on Strengthening Administration of Court Trials	SPC [2011] No. 2
51	Notice of the Supreme People's Court on Issuing Several Opinions on Further Strengthening Infrastructure Construction of Grass-roots People's Courts Under New Circumstances	SPC [2011] No. 4
52	Notice of the Supreme People's Court on Issuing Opinions on Strengthening People's Courts' Law Enforcement	SPC [2011] No. 11
53	Notice of the General Office of The Supreme People's Court on Issuing Basic Requirements of Trial Court Informatization	SPC-GO [2011] No. 18
54	Notice of the General Office of The Supreme People's Court on Issuing Further Strengthening Security Management of National Court Office Network	SPC-GO [2011] No. 89
55	Notice of the General Office of The Supreme People's Court on Issuing Opinions on Strengthening the Role of Judicial Functions in Providing Judicial Guarantee for Deepening Reform of Science and Technology System and Accelerating Construction of National Innovation System	SPC [2012] No. 15
56	Notice of the Supreme People's Court on Issuing Strengthening Work on Judicial Suggestions	SPC [2012] No. 74
57	Notice of the Supreme People's Court on Issuing Technical Specifications of Remote Video Interrogation Room Construction	SPC [2013] No. 48
58	Provisions of the Supreme People's Court on People's Courts' Publishing ruling documents on Internet	SPC-E [2013] No. 26
59	Notice of the General Office of The Supreme People's Court on Issuing The Interim Measures for People's Courts' Publishing ruling documents Concerning Intellectual Property on Internet	SPC-GO [2013] No. 102
60	Notice of the Supreme People's Court on Issuing A Five-Year Development Plan for the Information Construction of the People's Courts (2013-2017)	SPC [2013] No. 235
61	Opinions of the Supreme People's Court on Enhancing the Role of Trial Function and Promoting the Development of National New-type Urbanization	SPC [2014] No. 20
62	Notice of the Supreme People's Court on Issuing Provisions of Strengthening Court Leading Cadres' Research	SPC [2014] No. 10

SN	Title of document	Document No.
63	Notice of the Supreme People's Court on Issuing Several Opinions on the Publicity of Court Execution Procedure	SPC [2014] No. 18
64	Several Opinions of the Supreme People's Court on Consolidating the People's Courts' Practice in the New Situation Court Work Under New Circumstances	SPC [2014] No. 21
65	Guiding Opinions of the Supreme People's Court on the Construction of Court Litigation Service Center	SPC [2014] No. 23
66	Notice of the Supreme People's Court on Issuing Opinions on Issues Concerning Case Filing and Case Closing	SPC [2014] No. 26
67	Opinions of the Supreme People's Court on Protecting Non-public Sectors of Economy and Promoting its Healthy Development Equally in Accordance with Law	SPC [2014] No. 27
68	Notice of the Supreme People's Court on Issuing Provisions on Remote Video Reception of The Supreme People's Court	SPC [2014] No. 86
69	Opinions of the Supreme People's Court on Further Strengthening Work on Court Information	SPC [2014] No. 164
70	Opinions of the Supreme People's Court on Further Strengthening Work on judiciary's Function of Conveniencing and Benefiting people	SPC [2014] No. 293
71	The Supreme People's Court on Overall Deepening the Reform of the People's Courts — An Outline of the Forth Five-year Reform of the People's Courts	SPC [2015] No. 3
72	Opinions on Launching the Reform of File Registration System	SPC [2015] No. 6
73	Opinions of the Supreme People's Court on the Role of People's Courts in Providing Judicial Service and Guarantee for One Belt And One Road	SPC [2015] No. 9
74	Notice of the Supreme People's Court on Issuing Implementing Measures of People's Courts for Provisions on Records of Judicial Workers' Case Inquiring and Responsibility	SPC [2015] No. 11
75	Several Opinions of the Supreme People's Court on Enhancing Judicial Function in Public Security Maintenance	SPC [2015] No. 12
76	Notice of the Supreme People's Court on Issuing Planning of Education and Training of National Courts (2015-2019)	SPC [2015] No. 77
77	Notice of the Supreme People's Court on Issuing Implementation Specification on Provisions of Guiding Work with Cases	SPC [2015] No. 130
78	Notice of the Supreme People's Court on Issuing A Five-Year Development Plan for the Information Construction of the People's Courts (2016-2020)	SPC [2016] No. 66
79	Notice of the General Office of the Supreme People's Court on Issuing A Five-Year Development Plan for the Information Construction of the People's Courts (2016-2020)	SPC-GO [2016] No. 34

*SPC: the Supreme People's Court; SPC-GO: General Office of SPC; SPC-A: Administrative Office of SPC; SPC-E: Judicial Explanation of SPC; SPC-J: Justice Department of SPC.

Appendixes 2: A Five-Year Development Plan for the Construction of the Information System of the People's Courts (2016-2020)

1. Current Situation ... 76

1.1 System Construction Situation ... 76

1.1.1 Information infrastructure linked by five net systems is available in the courts at all levels ... 76

1.1.2 Business applications centered on case information management have been fully extended ... 77

1.1.3 Concentrated data management based on case information has achieved a significant breakthrough ... 78

1.2 Situation of guarantee system construction ... 78

1.2.1 The security service oriented by the graded protection of information system is carried out step by step ... 78

1.2.2 The operation guarantee system has been initially constructed with emphases on infrastructure and applications ... 78

1.2.3 Professional information talents have been growing and improving in the practice ... 79

1.3 The Effects of Informatization ... 79

1.3.1 Informatization serves people and has earned a good social response ... 79

1.3.2 Informatization serves trial enforcement and improves judicial quality ... 80

1.3.3 Informatization serves judicial management and anticipates a good prospect ... 81

1.4 Analysis on major problems ... 81

1.4.1 Overall planning and top-level design in need ... 82

1.4.2 The infrastructure is challenged by the rapid development of various applications ... 82

1.4.3 The integration and business supporting ability of application systems need strengthening ... 82

1.4.4 There are many weak links in the concentrated information management and service ... 83

1.4.5 The problem of comparatively laggard guarantee system construction is more prominent ... 83

1.4.6 The effect of informatized applications has much room for improvement ... 83

2. Developmental demands ... 84

2.1 Demands on Business Development ... 85

2.1.1 People's diversified judicial demands need to be met ... 85

2.1.2 Judicial quality and efficiency need improving ... 85

2.1.3 The scientificity of judicial management needs improving ... 85

2.2 Demands on top-level design ... 85

2.3 Demands on system construction ... 86

2.3.1 Demands on information infrastructure construction ... 86

2.3.2 Demands on application construction ... 87

2.3.3 Demands for data management and service 88
2.4 Demands on guarantee systems........ 89
2.4.1 The construction of security system needs to be strengthened and security level needs to be improved........ 89
2.4.2 The maintenance ability needs to be strengthened, and maintenance quality needs to be improved........ 89
2.4.3 The talent team construction needs to be accelerated as an intellectual support........ 89
2.5 Demands for the improvement of application efficacy 90

3. Guiding ideology, development concepts and construction targets........ 91
3.1 The Guiding Ideology 91
3.2 Development concepts 91
3.2.1 Centering on "One Goal" 91
3.2.2 Adhering to "Three Services"........ 91
3.2.3 Focusing on "Four Areas" 92
3.2.4 Highlighting "Six Features" 93
E. Realizing "Two-step Leaps" 94
3.3 Construction Targets........ 94

4. Major tasks 96
4.1 Strengthening top-level design under the guidance of the five-year development plan 96
4.2 Accelerating system construction focusing on expansion and integration........ 97
4.2.1 Integrated information infrastructures with all elements are to be constructed, supported by cloud computing 97
4.2.2 All-business and whole-process business application platforms are to be built with the focus on one-stop services........ 99
4.2.3 A smart service system of information resources is to be constructed to enhance "data management" capability 103
4.3 The guarantee systems are to be strengthened in line with the system construction and application demands........ 104
4.4 To enhance application effect through vigorous promotion and effect evaluation 106

5. Guarantee measures 108
5.1 Unifying thoughts and strengthening organization and leadership 108
5.2 Cultivating excellent information talents and enhancing the team strength 108
5.3 Increasing investment of funds and optimizing resource allocation 108
5.4 Intensifying science and technology research and realizing innovation-driven development 109
5.5 Enhancing the strict management of construction with systematic methods 109
5.6 Strengthening anti-corruption consciousness and constructing the information system in accordance with law and regulations 110

Fig. 1 An ever green tree of informatization of the people's court Version 2 111

Fig. 2 Framework of the people's court business 112

Fig. 3 Target of informatization of the people's court – Informatization standardization construction 113

Fig. 4 Target of informatization – Infrastructure construction 114

Fig. 5 Target of informatization – Application construction 115
Fig. 6 Target of informatization – Information resources construction 116
Fig. 7 Target of informatization of courts – Big data services 117
Fig. 8 Target of informatization – operation maintenance guarantee system 118
Fig. 9 An ever green tree of informatization of the people's courts Version 3.0 119
Fig. 10 A general framework of the informatization of the people's courts 120

Since the Eighteenth Party Congress, courts at all levels have been studying and applying the spirit of Xi Jinping's speeches, and made much progress in the construction of infrastructure, application systems, data resources and security, by centering on the layout of the "four comprehensives", aiming at the modernization of the judicial system and judicial ability, adhering to serving the people, trial enforcement and judicial management, and emphasizing the promotion of informatization, thus provided a strong support to the deepening of justice for the people, the improvement of judicial quality and efficiency, and the standardization of judicial management. Practice has proved that court informatization helps in promoting the national legal system construction, consolidating and deepening the achievements of judicial reforms, enhancing the judicial credibility of the courts, supporting and promoting the transformation and upgrading of economics, enriching and perfecting social credit system, and improving China's influence in global political and economic governance.

Now that the 12th five-year plan for national socioeconomic development has been successfully completed, the 13th five-year plan will be fully launched. The CPC central committee's strategy of law-based governance has given an important and divine mission to the people's court; the deepening of judicial reforms has given a strong driving force to the development of the court; a new global revolution of science and technology has provided a solid base of its informatization; and people's growing judicial demands have put forward an unprecedented demand for diversity in court work. To adapt to the situation and seize the opportunity, better coordinate and guide the court informatization at different levels during the five-year plan period, further promote the transformation and upgrading, and promote the modernization of judicial system and judicial ability, this program is formulated, on the basis of *The CPC Central Committee's Advice on the 13th Five-year Plan for National Economic and Social Development, Opinions of the Supreme People's Court on comprehensively Deepening the Reform of the People's Courts, A Plan for Government Informatization during the 13th Five-year Period* and other related documents.

1. Current Situation

During the 12th five-year period, particularly since the 18th Party Congress, informatization work has flourished and the Version 2.0 of court informatization system featured by interconnection has been basically constructed, supported by the "Tianping Project", with an efficient promotion of People's Supreme Court and initiative action of the courts at all levels.

1.1 System Construction Situation

The information system of the people's court has become a thriving evergreen tree (see figure 1). It has formed an interconnected and relatively fully categorized information infrastructure, linked by office intranet, private court network, court extranet, public network and secrecy-involving intranet. Ten business applications are available at all levels of courts, providing a direct support for judicial service, trial enforcement and judicial management; three information resources of judicial personnel, administrative information and trial enforcement as the main body have taken shape; concentrated data management has achieved a breakthrough and laid a good foundation for the construction of the Version 3.0 of data-centered court informatization system.

1.1.1 Information infrastructure linked by five net systems is available in the courts at all levels.

The infrastructures based on office network and private court network have become a main support of court informatization. Office network has been built in all courts, with access to private court network. The basic construction of the network environments, like network devices, computing devices, storage devices and system software, has been practically completed. The video conference system is widely available. The systems of technical court, remote arraignment and remote petition reception have covered the court system nationwide. Standardized computer rooms and the digital conference system have been built in some courts. The enforcement command centers have been built in 21 high courts, and information management centers built in 17.

The facilities of internet access and service fully support the courts in serving the masses. All the courts have internet access. Higher court websites and internet publishing platforms like judicial publicity have been built or joined up. Internet application has been moved to public clouds in a few areas, which is a support to the thriving development of internet application and mobile application.

The court extranet becomes an important channel for information sharing and business collaboration with related departments. The Supreme People's Court has established point-to-point connections with the Central Political and Judiciary Commission, Central Commission for Discipline Inspection, Government Affairs Administration, State Asset Regulatory Commission, Ministry of Finance, Supreme People's Procuratorate, Ministry of Public Security and other institutions, and established comprehensive connections with more than 20 banking and financial institutions, airline institutions and railway departments. 23 high courts have established point-to-point or comprehensive connections with relevant institutions by using special line or local e-government network, which basically meets the cooperative need in information distribution, information sharing, enforcement supervision, credit punishment and so on.

Secrecy-involving intranet construction has been started. (Omitted)

1.1.2 Business applications centered on case information management have been fully extended

The application system for judicial service like three judicial publicity platforms and the 3-in-one litigation service is being constantly enriched. Judicial publicity is encouraged by courts at all levels. The jurisdictionally unified platform for judicial process publicity has been built in all high courts, and is linked to the net of China's Trial Process Online. The platforms of judicial document publicity and enforcement information publicity have been built in the Supreme People's Court, which is shared by all courts. The 3-in-one litigation service (litigation service hall, litigation service network and 12368 litigation service hotline) center and lawyer service platform have been built in some courts, which support litigants' and lawyers' online participation in litigation. The courts at all levels have enriched their new medias and mobile service channels like websites, microbloggings, WeChat, mobile TV and so on.

The application system for trial enforcement has covered all the core practical processes. 99% of the courts have constructed case information management system, and realized the informatized support and management of important judicial processes. The system of enforcement information management has been constructed in the courts at all levels, and the systems of enforcement command, enforcement supervision and credit punishment have been constructed in most high courts and some intermediate and grass-roots courts. Remote video petition reception system and letter-petition management system have been constructed in all courts, and online appeal and letter-petition system has been constructed in some courts. The national library of the people's court branches, national legal knowledge database and document exchange system have been deployed in the private court network and are applicable in the four levels of courts. Trial systems like documents checking, risk assessment, case guidance and sentencing reference are to be constantly enriched. The mobile office working system has been in operation in some areas.

The application systems for judicial management like personnel management and general administration are promoted steadily from the top down. More than 90% of courts have constructed personnel management system, and more than 50% constructed administration systems and internal websites. The exploratory construction of information system supporting unified personnel, finance and property management, people's assessor management, judge selection and other work has been started in some judicial reform pilot areas.

1.1.3 Concentrated data management based on case information has achieved a significant breakthrough

Concentrated data management platform has realized nationwide coverage of court case information. Concentrated court data management platform has been built. The concentrated data management of all the cases from 3,512 courts and the convergence of personnel data in some courts have been realized. Mechanisms of data transmission, updating and maintenance have been established, and 94.7% of courts have realized the real-time submission of case data, 80% realized real-time information updates for case registration, case division, court session, process transition and case settlement, and nearly 70% realized daily updating of adjudicative document information.

The court case information transmission and exchange has been realized based on private court networks. Data transmission and exchange system has been constructed at high courts and above, and provinces have realized the data uploading and exchange between jurisdictional intermediate and grass-roots courts by various technical means. The level-by-level submission of court case information to the Supreme People's Court has been realized.

The special analysis and service of judicial data have achieved initial success. The integration and mining of national trial data has been preliminarily developed, and the service of judicial statistics analysis, judicial quality and efficiency analysis, specific item analysis and information search is offered. The in-depth analysis of social hotspots and concerned similar cases is attempted for the pre-judgement of emerging problems.

1.2 Situation of guarantee system construction

The guarantee system for court informatization is being constructed steadily, with emphases on safety, maintenance and talents, and has offered a strong support for the construction and application of information system.

1.2.1 The security service oriented by the graded protection of information system is carried out step by step

(Omitted).

1.2.2 The operation guarantee system has been initially constructed with emphases on infrastructure and applications

Outsourcing has become a main mode for infrastructure operation and maintenance. 168 million yuan has been spent on its operation every year by courts at all levels, and permanent outsourcing technicians for maintenance have amounted to 1400 people. 70% of high courts have regulated infrastructure operation and maintenance, and 60% have application maintenance.

Maintenance work is being extended to data and security. 50% of high courts have data maintenance by self-support or outsourcing, and some courts in places like Beijing have security maintenance by outsourcing.

Visualized maintenance has become an effective means for the control of information system operation. 50% of high courts have realized visualized infrastructure maintenance. Problems are detected and solved in advance through the dynamic monitoring of various equipment, and the stable operation of information system is ensured.

1.2.3 Professional information talents have been growing and improving in the practice

Information technology organizations provide a basic guarantee for the informatization. The leading group for the construction of informatization has been organized in the courts at all levels. The Supreme People's Court has set up information center, the high courts have set up IT departments, and some intermediate and grass-roots courts have set up special institutions or employed professional office IT talents.

Professional information talents have become an important part of judicial ancillary team. The Supreme People's Court issued *Opinions on the Team Construction of Information Personnel in the People's Courts* in June 2015, clearly claiming that information talents should be incorporated into judicial ancillary team, and putting forward requirements for the configuration of institutions and professional structures.

A professional technological team of about 7,200 people has been formed, with more than 5,300 permanent staff and over 1,900 contract-based employees in all courts. The professional quality of the team is being improved through a variety of ways such as technical training, cross-regional communication, topic-specific lectures and special workshops.

1.3 The Effects of Informatization

The informatization of court work has had a remarkable effects in promoting judicial publicity, deepening judicial service for the people, improving trial quality and regulating judicial management. It has won the full recognition of the Party Central Committee, the central politics and law committee, court policemen and the vast majority of people.

1.3.1 Informatization serves people and has earned a good social response

The depth and width of judicial publicity is expanded. Based on the three platforms of judicial publicity and the new court media, all the courts coordinate the work and carry it forward simultaneously. The diversified judicial demands of the masses are basically met, and their rights of information, participation, expression and supervision are guaranteed. People are enabled to know information that is more real and symmetric, understanding that all the public information has been publicized and that the judge is taking an impartial position. An organic unity of the cases' social effect and legal effect is preliminarily achieved.

The field and window of judicial service is opened up. Based on the 3-in-one litigation service (litigation service hall, litigation service network and 12368 litigation service hotline) platform, an interactive, fully covered and multi-dimensional litigation service like online case registration, electronic service, live trial, document query and file inquiry is offered. The active notification of important information, real-time query and active response to questions have been realized, and the ability of diversified judicial service (online and offline service, in-court and out-of-court service) has been achieved. People spend less time on the way, less money, and have less troubled. Judicature is closer to people.

The means and channels of public communication are innovated. Convenient communication channels are established, taking advantage of new medias like government affairs websites, mobile phone APPs, "microblog" gings, WeChat and micro-videos for their real-time interaction and wide audience. Real-time interaction between the clients and courts is enabled. Information is obtained on needs, and a participation in communication is possible at any time. Laws are interpreted by cases, law-ruling culture is transmitted, law-ruling spirit is carried on, and the judicial functions of social education, guidance and regulation are exercised. Meanwhile, the social supervision of people from all walks of life is accepted, which is a driving force for the judicial personnel to improve their judicial ability and quality.

1.3.2 Informatization serves trial enforcement and improves judicial quality

The contradiction between judicial demands and judicial ability is resolved. Online circulation of node information in major trial procedures and digitalized file management have been realized, based on the system of case information management, and the routinization of trial work is promoted. Trial supporting services such as law query, case guidance, judgment reference, one-click editing and intelligent correction are offered. Based on the trial supporting system, and case handling becomes more convenient and efficient for judges. People spend less time rushing about, and the costs of litigation and judicature are reduced, due to the systems of electronic signature, remote court hearing and so on.

Strict justice is ensured through whole-process tracing and supervision. Depending on the characteristics and advantage of information technology in whole-process tracing and dynamic tracking, case handling duration is early warned, case handling procedures supervised, case handling risk estimated, and judicial behaviors inspected. Important parts, important points, important positions and members are supervised and restricted in the implementation of judicial power and executive power. Main judicial behaviors are dynamically monitored to prevent the abuse of judicial power. Illicit case handling is left nowhere to hide, which has played a positive role in regulating judicial power, promoting judicial justice and enhancing judicial credibility.

Judicial process reengineering and business innovation is promoted. The enforcement command system is formed, four levels of courts as an organic whole, internal and external work highly linked. Exposure of dishonest persons subject to enforcement, property check and control, and credit penalties are intensified, to force dishonest persons subject to enforcement to obey court decisions because of the power of joint credit penalties. Four levels of courts receive petitions interactively through remote video, which functions positively in reducing litigation-related Beijing visits and solving letter-petition difficulties. Jilin courts have innovated "internet +" litigation services, allowing people to participate in judicial processes through online interaction; The whole litigation process, including case registration, fee collection, evidence exchange, paper examining, and even the court session, can be handled online.

1.3.3 Informatization serves judicial management and anticipates a good prospect

Real-time and dynamic command of the courts' judicial situation is made possible. 63 million case data and 34 million judicative documents in the past four years have been gathered in the courts' centralized data management platform, with an average daily increase of 50,000 to 60,000 cases. Based on this, analyses on case filing and closing, judicial quality and efficiency, hot issues and type-specific cases are carried out for a full reflection of the courts' judicial dynamic, quality and efficiency.

The case handling service for judges becomes smarter. The big database provides a support for judges in the query and reference for similar cases. Accurate investigation of the truth and correct application of laws are guaranteed. Uncertainty and subjectivity in judicial judgements and decisions are reduced, which promotes agreement of judicial standards. The dynamic case management such as assistant case division, stage-specific items, case nature adjustment and specialized collegial panel is supported, and the effect and standard of judicial management is improved. Some courts even merge personnel information and trial information, to command the real-time trial management, evaluate the judges' personal performance, improve the efficiency of judicial personnel management, and promote the judges' self-discipline, self-evaluation and self-management.

Judicial reform and business innovation are assisted. External information resources such as population database and lawyer database help in solving problems in litigation service like identity authentication. Scattered data are put together, and the analyses of all the data help in capturing people's judicial demands and judging judicial situation, and also provide a basis for the adjustment and optimization of judicial policies and measures. Online and offline resources are integrated to promote the reform of trial mode and make informationization advanced productivity.

1.4 Analysis on major problems

With the ever-deepening of informatization construction and the generalization of applications, some deep-rooted problems in the work are gradually revealed.

1.4.1 Overall planning and top-level design in need

The guidance of development planning over informatization construction is relatively weak. The construction plan and implementation of the "Tianping Project" diverge to a certain extent. Unified technical standards for informatization construction are needed. A mature evaluation index system for the effectiveness of the construction is in need. Informatization construction needs a targeted preliminary study on the core technology and key technology. A comprehensive management system for informatization construction has not been constructed. Applications like electronic service lack relevant legal support.

1.4.2 The infrastructure is challenged by the rapid development of various applications

The private court network has not all succeeded in sending people's courts to "the last kilometer". Network bandwidth shortage becomes a common problem for the private networks in different places, though varying in degree. Computing and storage equipment cannot meet the increasing court business demands. It is difficult to crosslink audio and video systems. The interconnection of court extranets with related institutions remains absent. Internet computing, internet storage, and the self-building and self-maintaining of network equipment becomes more and more difficult. Private mobile networks have not been in large-scale operalion yet. The internetwork information exchange is low in efficiency, and cannot fully support business coordination.

1.4.3 The integration and business supporting ability of application systems need strengthening

Various application systems urgently need function integration and information integration to support the converging and sharing. Internal court work platforms and external service applications are not coordinating efficiently, and litigation service lack unified entrance and integrated service. Case information management system still cannot fully meet the trial enforcement requirements set by *Opinions of the Supreme People's Court on Comprehensively Deepening the Reform of the People's Courts*, and cannot fully support the business coordination between higher and lower courts, between jurisdictionally different courts, and between courts and related governmental institutions. Site-wide business application and the ability of trial supporting system in assisting judges' trial management are both inadequate, thus have not provided a strong support for grass-roots courts in solving the imbalance between case and personnel numbers. Mobile case handling, electronic document exchange and archives management ability need improving. Traditional personnel management system cannot fully meet the demands of judicial reform in the unified personnel, finance and property management, and the dynamic judicial position adjustment. The construction of application systems for administrative affairs management is not balanced and remains absent in some courts.

1.4.4 Wany weak links in the concentrated information management and service still exist

The ranges of data collection in different high courts are irregular, and external data on judicial affairs, judicial research and informatized management, as well as other related judicial data, have not been input into the judicial information database. The quality of collected case data needs improving. The system of data sharing and exchanging between higher and lower courts, between courts and other departments, and between different networks has not been fully established yet. The intelligence level of big data analysis is not sufficient to provide fully covered and high-level service for populace litigation, law dissemination, judicial resource allocation, social management and public service.

1.4.5 The problem of comparatively laggard guarantee system construction is more prominent

The information security systems in courts at all levels need to keep up with the times. Various business applications still lack unified identity authentication mechanism. The organizational structure and service mode of the operation and maintenance system are not perfect; the unified control ability over the information system has not been formed yet; data operation and security maintenance have not been carried out fully. The supporting capability of the informatization talents needs improving.

1.4.6 The effect of informatized applications has much room for improvement

The effect of sunny judicature has not reached the expected level. The application popularization and people's satisfaction of the three judicial publicity platforms need much improvement, and the one-stop judicial service ability for varied participants is still not powerful. The available applications of trial enforcement are far from easy to use, and some have even, to some extent, increased the burden of the judges. Data collection and the integrity, accuracy and timeliness of statistics cannot meet the court police's demands. The applications for administrative affairs management still cannot meet the demands of various business departments. The achievements of court informatization construction are applied and popularized with various channels, narrow range of coverage, and deficient focalization. The concept of stressing construction and neglecting application is common. Ideas and methods for the evaluation of informatization construction achievements are lacking. An effective mechanism for the evaluation, report and improvement of the application effects has not been constructed.

2. Developmental demands

The construction of court informatization is facing both rare opportunities and unprecedented urgent demands in the new period.

The mission of informatization in serving the national law-ruling strategy is becoming ever more demanding. The construction of a sunny judicial system that is open, dynamic, transparent and convenient was proposed in the Fourth Plenary Session by the 18th CPC Central Committee. Informatization is not only an important support for the strengthening of judicial management and the improvement of judicial efficiency, but also an inevitable choice in the deepening of judicial publicity and enhancement of judicial credibility. It requires courts at all levels to look at informatization construction from a wider perspective of overall promotion of law-based governance, to put informatization into all the businesses, dimensions and processes of court work, and to lead the modernization of court work through informatization.

The task of informatization to serve people's judicial demands becomes more urgent. Information technology is developing rapidly, and people's judicial demands have presented new characteristics. New demands are put forward in the comprehensiveness of information, distance in communication and immediacy of interaction, which requires all courts to focus on informatization construction to meet people's diversified judicial demands, respond actively to people's concerns, broaden the new channels of justice for people, and deepen new measures for judicial publicity.

The responsibility of informatization to serve judicial reforms becomes more onerous. 65 judicial reforms from 7 aspects are proposed in *Opinions of the Supreme People's Court on Comprehensively Deepening the Reform of the People's Courts*, among which 35 reforms rely directly on information technology. The construction of court informatization is not only a basic component of judicial reform, but also an important engine and driving force of it. This requires the courts at all levels to plan the informatization construction within a greater scheme of judicial reform, and solve the realistic problems and development difficulties in work through modern information technology.

The opportunity of informatization to serve the courts' scientific development is priceless. Network Strategy, "Internet +" action plan and national big data strategy were proposed in the fifth plenary session by the 18th CPC central committee. Modern information technology is constantly infiltrating and influencing all aspects of court work. Under the premise of adhering to the rules of judicial work, transformation and upgrading are the trend of the times. They require all the courts to promote informatization construction to grasp the development opportunities, and require them to insist on the drive for innovation, take a head start in technology, and promote the in-depth fusion of new tech with court work, to offer inexhaustible strength for the transformation and upgrading of court informatization.

2.1 Demands on Business Development

2.1.1 People's diversified judicial demands need to be met

The width and depth of judicial publicity need to be expanded to make the masses understand that all public information has been publicized. Whole-process and integrated litigation service should be offered to the participants to lessen their trouble and reduce their litigation cost. More convenient communication channels need to be established for a better supervision from the society and a more timely and comprehensive interaction between people and the courts.

2.1.2 Judicial quality and efficiency need improving

According to *Opinions of the Supreme People's Court on Comprehensively Deepening the Reform of the People's Courts*, online trial business should be fully realized with whole-process tracing and real-time dynamic monitoring. Judges should be assisted in the improvement of reasoning ability in judicial documents, by such means as case reference. And their needs for outside case-handling should be met. For enforcement business, the management of process nodes needs strengthening, the systems for enforcement supervision and credit penalty need improving, and an integrated, interactive, regulated and efficient enforcement system needs to be constructed. And for the letter-petition business, the system for the closure of lawsuit-related letter-petitions should be improved, and a system for in-place petition reception and supervision should be constructed. The unified management by the four levels of courts is to be realized. Front-line trial judges should be supported in the improvement of work efficiency.

2.1.3 The scientificity of judicial management needs improving

The situation, characteristics and regularity of trial enforcement need to be analyzed to provide legislative suggestions, judicial suggestions and policy-making references for social governance and social economic development. The standardization, specialization and professionalization of court personnel need to be promoted. Sort judicial personnel management, judicial post management, judge election management and judge performance evaluation system need to be constructed and improved to realize the dynamic management and all-round supervision and evaluation of the judge work. Unified online retrieval and transfer of litigation files among nationwide courts need to be promoted to improve the level of litigation archive management.

2.2 Demands on top-level design

For top-level design as the weakest link in court informatization construction, the leading role of development planning should be played to the full. All work of top-level design need to be strengthened from the source of business demands (see figure 2) in informatization construction. A practicable five-year development plan need to be formulated and adjusted yearly to better coordinate the informatization construction among jurisdictional courts. An overall designing of the informatization construction in jurisdictional courts needs to be made based on the five-year development plan, specifying construction requirements and technical scheme, and coordinating project development. Existing standards in different places need to be integrated as soon as possible. Standardized management system and working mechanism needs to be improved. A standard system of court informatization needs to be constructed and improved (see figure 3). An evaluation index system for informatization applications needs to be constructed to cover all the main court businesses nationwide and to be amended and perfected in practice. Preliminary studies and technology research need to be carried out, specifically on the key technologies that affect judicial management and judicial ability, to support the rapid development of court informatization. A management mechanism covering the main businesses, working processes and asset elements in the construction and applications of court informatization need to be built. Proposals of legislative modification need to be put forward to support such applications as electronic service.

2.3 Demands on system construction

In view of the growing business demands and increasing performance requirements of court informatization, information infrastructure needs further improving; various business applications need to be developed; and data management and service need to be strengthened.

2.3.1 Demands on information infrastructure construction

The five net systems need to be improved and optimized. A private mobile network needs to be built, and the five net systems of private court network, private mobile network, court extranet, internet, and secrecy-involving intranet need to be constructed. Private cloud, open cloud and secrecy cloud of the courts need to be constructed through the integration of the systems. Key infrastructures such as litigation service, trial enforcement and judicial management need to be integrated for the construction of integrated information infrastructure (see figure 4).

(1) Private cloud needs to be constructed based on the private court network and related key infrastructure

Technical structures needs to be optimized according to the demands of various data and audio/video applications. The coverage of the private network needs expanding and the performance of private network functions need improving to support the flexible business deployment. The construction of information management center needs to be strengthened to realize the unified information scheduling and management. The construction of litigation service hall needs to be regulated to realize multifunctional one-stop litigation service. The integrated audio/video management platform needs to be built for the linkup and display of various business videos. The construction of technical courts needs to be promoted to meet the requirements for trial recording and reexamining. Data backup system needs to be constructed for data safety. Computer Rooms need to be renewed, built or rented according to the standardization requirements. A digital conference system needs to be constructed to meet the requirements in the information age. A private mobile network needs to be built to support the outside mobile businesses such as mobile officing, circuit trial and dispatched enforcement. The connection of court extranet needs to be developed and improved to support the information exchange, information sharing and business collaboration with different institutions.

(2) Constructing an open cloud of courts through social services

A higher demand has therefore to be formulated for computing, storage and network, in a constant growth in internet-based operations of courts, for a more exhaustive use of social resources, and for a comprehensive improvement of the supporting capability of the court operation on internet by constructing open court cloud on the rentals of public cloud, and by implementing flexible operation and resources, controllable costs in accordance with needs, and stable operation of the system. It is also possible to make full use of the state e-government net for supporting the open judicial operations.

(3) Court secrecy-involving cloud needs to be constructed through national e-government intranet.

(Omitted).

2.3.2 Demands on application construction

Existing applications need to be integrated to cover all businesses and all processes, and to provide a one-stop service platform the for people and the court police (see Fig. 5).

(1) Convenience applications need to be enriched and integrated to meet people's diverse judicial demands.

The judicial open platform needs to be renewed to perfect such functions as information query and case association. The platform of whole-process litigation service should be constructed to provide one-stop litigation service for the people. A nationally unified 12368 litigation service system should be constructed, with speech and message service. The government affairs websites should be integrated; new medias and mobile application should be enriched; and more convenient communication channels should be built, to make judicial publicity and litigation reach all the courts and people.

(2) Trial enforcement applications need to be integrated and perfected to improve trial quality and efficiency

Trial, enforcement, letter-petition, and their convergence with judicial service applications should be vigorously promoted on the basis of various existing applications. Meanwhile, according to the requirements of judicial reform and *Standards of People's Court Informatization (2015)*, trial business system needs to be upgraded and perfected, the monitor of trial nodes to be reinforced, litigation archive management to be strengthened, trial quality evaluation to be improved, trial supporting system to be perfected, and judicial statistics to be automatically generated, to support the business coordination between the higher and lower level courts, jurisdictionally different courts and related governmental institutions. The judicial process information and file publicity need to be promoted, the range of list system and joint punishments on dishonest persons subject to enforcement to be widened, and the mode of online judicial auction carried forward. Remote petition reception and letter-petition management need to be perfected to realize nationally unified management of letter-petition work. The businesses of officing and case handling should reach mobile terminal.

(3) The application of judicial management need to be expanded and strengthened to meet the demand for improved scientificity of government affairs management

A private website connecting four levels of courts need to be built to realize the top-down transmission and multilaterial communication of information. The personnel management system needs to be improved to meet the judicial reform demands such as personnel management and judge performance evaluation. The judicial administration management system needs to be perfected to cover such businesses as administrative affairs, archive management, legal research and judicial assistance, and to be integrated with the personnel system to meet the demands for unified personnel, finance and property management in sub-provincial courts.

2.3.3 Demands for data management and service

Based on the platform of concentrated court data management, information resources need to be integrated; exchange capacity to be strengthened; and the level of intelligent service to be enhanced.

(1)The range of data collection need to be extended and the judicial information database to be perfected

Various data in all the courts, such as judicial enforcement, judicial personnel, judicial affairs, judicial studies and informatized management, need to be integrated, in view of the problems of incomplete data collection and low data quality. Related external data resources need to be introduced to realize the nationwide coverage of judicial information resources (see Fig. 6).

(2) A shared exchange system needs to be constructed to support data integration and interconnection.

In view of the vertically disconnected and laterally unshared data, a unified and shared exchange system needs to be constructed to realize the cross-system, cross-departmental, cross-regional, multi-level and cross-network data share. As a response to the low data association between different systems, judicial data need to be associated based on "person", "case" and "thing", to realize data convergence.

(3) Big data analysis system needs to be constructed and various intelligent services need to be developed

Big data analysis system need to be constructed to realize the multiple retrieval and in-depth analysis of nationwide judicial information resources and to support timely, accurate and dynamic intelligent services (see Fig. 7). Based on the system, the judicial openness and intelligent litigation services need to be offered for the people, to provide policy-making support and intelligent monitoring and early-warning services for the trial enforcement, and to provide intelligent services of judicial research and performance evaluation for judicial management.

2.4 Demands on guarantee systems

The construction of guarantee systems for safety, maintenance and talents needs to be strengthened in response to the situation and demands of the rapid court informatization construction.

2.4.1 The construction of security system needs to be strengthened and security level needs to be improved

(Omitted).

2.4.2 The maintenance ability needs to be strengthened, and maintenance quality needs to be improved

A high-quality and efficient maintenance management system (see Fig. 8) needs to be constructed based on the court actuality and referring to relevant maintenance standards at home and abroad. 100% infrastructure, application systems, data management and information security are to be dynamically monitored. The management mode of emergency maintenance aimed at equipment reliability needs to be changed. Through the construction of visualized operation platform, functions such as the dynamic monitoring, malfunction prevention and effectiveness evaluation of the information system are to be realized, and the maintenance quality and efficiency is to be comprehensively improved. Emergency responding platform and emergency safeguard mechanism of the information system need to be built to improve the guarantee ability in emergencies.

2.4.3 The talent team construction needs to be accelerated as an intellectual support

The organizational guarantee mechanism for informatization needs to be improved. The function of leading groups for informatization at different levels of courts is to be fully effectuated, and coordinative guidance to be strengthened. A professional advisory team need to be built, to provide technical support to the society. A scientific specialty classification system needs to be built for the formation of professional management and technical talent teams. Types of professionalized personnel need to be complete and strong. The channels for the promotion of professionals are to be perfected, with an emphasis on practice and exercise, to bring a good mechanism for talent cultivation. The construction of information is to be accelerated healthily.

2.5 Demands for the improvement of application efficacy

The concept and situation of "emphasizing construction while neglecting application" needs to be changed. The improvement of application efficacy should be an important task of informatization. An effective mechanism for the evaluation, report and improvement of application efficacy should be built, to make the enhancement of application efficacy really visible, quantifiable, assessable and evaluable. The advocating and training mechanisms of the informatization achievements should be built, to gradually set up the brand image of court informatization and improve people's recognition and satisfaction. The application ability of informatization among the judges and personnel in courts at all levels need to be enhanced, and the improvement of application efficacy of informatization needs to be promoted.

3. Guiding ideology, development concepts and construction targets

3.1 The Guiding Ideology

The Guiding ideology is to implement the development concept of "innovation, coordination, green, open and sharing", center on the strategic plan of law-based governance, aim at the modernization of judicial system and judicial ability, adhere to the service for the masses, trial enforcement and judicial administration, strengthen the top-level design, accelerate system construction, reinforce the guarantee system, improve application efficacy, construct the overall covering, mobile and interconnected, cross-sectorial, thoroughly applied, transparent and convenient, and safe and controllable court informatization Version 3.0 along the stepped pathway from overall construction to further amelioration, and to provide a powerful information and technology guarantee for the work of court informatization.

3.2 Development concepts

The main development concept is to implement "13462" (the following items) general thought and promote the transformation and upgrading of court informatization.

3.2.1 Centering on "One Goal"

The court informatization Version 3.0 (see Fig. 9 and Fig. 10) is to be constructed, aimed at promoting the modernization of judicial system and judicial capability. Smart courts that support online all-business handling, publicity of whole-process trial enforcement elements and comprehensive smart service for judges, litigation participants, the public and governmental institutions are to be formed.

3.2.2 Adhering to "Three Services"

To meet judicial demands and serve target users is always the fundamental starting point of informatization construction.

Informatization is to serve the people. The judicial service of "routinized judicial publicity, integrated litigation service and diversified legal advocacy" is to be initiatively offered to the people, by keeping to the construction of a sunny judicial mechanism that is open, dynamic, transparent and convenient, driven by the people-profited service requirements in "Internet +" action plan, and through informatization channels of judicial publicity, litigation service, legal advocacy, supervision suggestions and so on.

Informatization is to serve trial enforcement. Aimed at the enhancement of trial quality and efficiency and the guarantee of judicial justice, the applications of trial enforcement are to be provided to the police in convenient use, coordinated businesses and intelligent services; through the informatization construction of judicial business, enforcement business, appeal and letter-petition, judicial management and judicial assistance, to enhance the service ability for trial enforcement and judicial assistance.

Informatization is to serve judicial administration. Guided by the concept of "big data, large scale, and great service", informatized applications are to be actively extended to administrative fields such as administrative affairs, archive management, personnel management, discipline inspection, financial management and logistics equipment, to provide assistant management means of "integrative data, visible process and precise management" and to practically improve the scientificity of judicial policies and management.

3.2.3 Focusing on "Four Areas"

The objective laws of informatization construction should be followed, and the promotion of court informatization should focus on four areas with both clear division of responsibility and mutual support.

Top-level designing is to be strengthened. In view of the generally weak coordinative planning and top-level design in court informatization, the top-level designing such as development planning, overall technical scheme, technical standard, evaluation index system, management mechanism and technology innovation should be strengthened to provide a scientific guidance for infromatizaiton.

The system construction is to be accelerated. Base on the vigorous development and remarkable achievements of court informatization, information infrastructure is to be further expanded, business applications are to be extended, information resource service is to be developed and the construction of various systems is to be integrated, to provide rich and thorough informatized application supports for the people and court police.

Guarantee system is to be strengthened. The guarantee elements such as organization system, management mechanism and technological means for information security, operation maintenance and talent teams are to be adjusted, enriched, improved and perfected, to provide a strong support for the development and construction, operation and application, resource accumulation and performance improvement of various information systems.

The application efficacy is to be improved. The old thought of "emphasizing construction while ignoring application" for informatization construction is to be practically changed, and the application efficacy of the informatization system in service of the people, trial enforcement and judicial management is to be collected, analyzed and evaluated as an important basis for the assessment of informatization construction and the perfection of information system, to further improve the application efficacy and user satisfaction of the court informatization construction.

3.2.4 Highlighting "Six Features"

The demands of court modernization construction and the trend of new information technology development are to be integrated to fully reflect the time features of court informatization.

Feature one: overall coverage. Through the full use of advanced network and cloud technology, to be effectuated are a full coverage of interconnected network of four levels of courts, a full coverage of businesses and processes of judicial trials, judicial personnel and judicial affairs, a full coverage of various judicial information resources and a full coverage of diversified judicial demands from litigants, social public and related governmental departments.

Feature two: mobile internet. Through the full use of mobile internet technology and active expansion of public mobile applications, judicial publicity and litigation services are to be offered to litigants, lawyers and the public anytime and anywhere. The applications such as circuit trial, enforcement and servicing, and private court network access are to be promoted. Mobile terminal applications such as officing and case handling are to be promoted steadily according to the requirements for information security, to provide optimized convenience for judges.

Feature three: cross-sectorial integration. Through the full use of cloud computing, sharing and exchanging technologies, various infrastructures, application systems and information resources are to be effectively integrated and expanded, to realize both the interconnection between different fields within the court system and the horizental fusion communication of the courts with related external institutions in network, information and businesses.

Feature four: in-depth application. Through the full use of rich judicial information resources and technologies such as big data, cloud computing, future networks and artificial intelligence, analyses are to be conducted on the operation situation, characteristics and regularities of trial enforcement under the new circumstances, to provide ever-deepening information decision services for the court construction as well as the state and social governance.

Feature five: Transparency and convenience. Through the full use of internet technology and on the basis of the three judicial open platforms, the breadth and depth of judicial openness is to be expanded, and judicial credibility to be enhanced. Judicial measures to serve and benefit people are to be innovated, to provide diversified, convenient and more humanized online and offline services for the litigants.

Feature six: security and controllability. Advanced information security technologies are to be fully used, the police's information security awareness to be enhanced, information security guarantee mechanism to be perfected, the requirements for hierarchical protection and graded protection be carried out, and the risk prevention and control ability of basic information networks and important information systems to be improved, to guarantee the synchronous development of information security and informatization construction.

E. Realizing "Two-step Leaps"

Based on the actual development of the courts nationwide, the construction of court informatization is to realize its two-step leaps from "overall completion" to "amelioration and perfection".

The first leap is to complete the construction of court informatization Version 3.0 by the end of 2017. The general framework that represents the world's advanced level of court informatization with Chinese characteristics will cover the courts nationwide. The construction and application of network infrastructure, business application system, and information resource management and service system, all with the "six features," will be demonstrated in some areas. And the application efficacy of "three services" will be significantly improved.

The second leap is to ameliorate and perfect the court informatization Version 3.0 nationwide by the end of 2020. The general frame will be optimized in operation and application. The construction and application of the network infrastructure, business application system, and information resource management and service system, with the "six features," will cover the courts nationwide. And the application efficacy of "three services" will be overall enhanced.

3.3 Construction Targets

Based on the scientific, reasonable and feasible top-level design, the court informatization system will be constructed nationwide by the end of 2017, while being centered around the data management platform, supported by private cloud and open cloud, linked by five net systems, focused on twenty three kinds of applications, and guaranteed by security, maintenance and talent teams. The main businesses will be 100% informatization in high courts and above, and the informatization of trial enforcement, judicial personnel and informatization management will reach 100% coverage in the national judicial information database. The diverse judicial demands from the litigants, the public and related governmental institutions will be basically covered. Private court network will reach all the court networks, and offer main business service for various users through mobile internet. The internet access to and information exchange with main external related institutions will be realized on demands. Higher degree of information sharing and business collaboration will be realized among the high (and above) courts and some intermediate courts. The intelligent big data service of the high (and above) courts and some intermediate courts will be able to support the main businesses such as litigation service, trial enforcement and judicial management. The courts at all levels will realize whole-process judicial publicity such as case registration, court hearing, trial enforcement, hearing process, judicial documents and judicial affairs. Convenience measures such as online petition reception, case registration, file service, evidence exchange, information query, judicial consultation and mediation will be promoted. And the people's satisfaction with the informatized service will reach 80% or above. The assessment and rectification of important information systems with level 3 (and above) maintenance will be overall completed. The guarantee system for infrastructures, applications, data maintenance and security maintenance will be improved, and the maintenance efficacy will be visualized. The teams of informatization talents will be built and perfected. The system for application effect evaluation will be basically formed and cover all the courts. The Chinese-featured court informatization Version 3.0 will be overall constructed and play a predominant role in the modernization of judicial system and judicial capability.

By the end of 2020, the top-level design of court informatization will be further enriched and perfected. The court informatization system, centered around big data management and service platforms, supported by the private cloud, open cloud and secrecy cloud, and focused on whole-process and all-business application platforms, will be extended to intermediate and grass-roots courts. The main businesses will be 100% informatized in intermediate courts (and above) and most grass-roots courts. And information of trial enforcement, judicial personnel, judicial affairs, judicial studies and informatization management will by 100% coverage in the national judicial information database. The access to internet and information exchange with related external institutions will be realized on demands. All-dimensional service will be offered for various users through mobile internet. All the courts will realize the information sharing and business collaboration between applications and data, internal and external, and management and service. The intelligent big data service of all the courts will fully support various businesses such as litigation service, trial enforcement and judicial management. The whole-process judicial publicity in all the courts, such as case registration, court hearing, trial enforcement, hearing process, ruling documents and judicial affairs, will be deepened and perfected. Convenience measures such as online petition reception, case registration, file service, evidence exchange, information query, judicial consultation and mediation will be generalized. People's satisfaction with the informatized service will reach 90% or above. The assessment and rectification of important non-secrecy information systems will be overall completed. The guarantee system for infrastructures, applications, data maintenance and security maintenance will be overall constructed, and the maintenance effects visualized. The informatization talent teams and management systems will be constantly improved in all courts. The system for application efficacy evaluation will all be perfected. The court informatization Version 3.0 will be continuously optimized to support the modernization of judicial system and judicial capability.

4. Major tasks

Fifty-five tasks in four categories need to be accomplished in the court informatization construction during the five-year plan period.

4.1 Strengthening top-level design under the guidance of the five-year development plan

The top-level design is to be guided and strengthened through year-by-year evaluation and amendment of the five-year development plan.

(1) To draw up and evaluate and amend yearly the five-year development plan

A five-year development plan for the informatization construction of national courts, the Supreme People's Court, and high courts and their jurisdictional courts is to be drawn up, and evaluated and amended year by year, to coordinate the informatization construction in different courts. Technical practice is to be guided, and funds input to be obtained.

(2) To design the overall technical scheme of the information construction

The design and scheme of the overall technical framework for the jurisdictional court informatization are to be effectuated according to the five-year development plan. Through the implementation of "Tianping Project", the schemes of system construction, guarantee system and performance improvement are to be specified, the construction work such as system research and development, data management and resource service to be supported, and interconnection and communication, information sharing and business collaboration between different systems, between different courts and between courts and external institutions to be guaranteed.

(3) To build and improve the standard system of the courts

The standardization of people's courts is to be promoted, and standardized management system and working mechanism to be improved. The existing standard systems for the courts are to be comprehensively revised and integrated by the Supreme People's Court, and relevant business standards to be perfected. The standard system for the court informatization is to be built, together with three types of standard specifications for infrastructure, technology and management. Local standard specifications are to be enriched by high courts, based on the needs of local judicial work and the features of local informatization construction.

(4) To build an evaluation index system for the court informatization

The Supreme People's Court is to build an evaluation index system for the court informatization, and set evaluation indexes for six aspects of construction, application, service, management, guarantee and performance. High courts are to specify local evaluation indexes regarding the actual work of local informatization.

(5) To implement IT innovation project in the court informatization

The Supreme People's Court is to organize and implement IT innovation project in the court informatization, carry out preliminary studies of core technologies and test research of key technologies, and build developing and testing platforms for court information technologies. High courts are encouraged to carry out technical innovations and local demonstration projects, to accumulate experience for technology generalization.

(6) To improve integrated management mechanism for court informatization

Court informatization management systems, such as appropriation budgets, procurement assessment, project construction, project supervision, project acceptance, asset management, intellectual rights, operation maintenance and performance evaluation, are to be perfected to improve investment benefit and construction efficiency. Legislative suggestions are to be proposed for the modification of laws and regulations supporting such applications as electronic delivery.

4.2 Accelerating system construction focusing on expansion and integration

On the basis of various existing information systems, business application supports are to be further expanded. Meanwhile, the interconnection and convergence of different systems are to be promoted, to improve the level of integration.

4.2.1 Integrated information infrastructures with all elements are to be constructed, supported by cloud computing

Private cloud, open cloud and secrecy cloud are to be built based on the private court network, private mobile network, court extranet, internet, and secrecy-involved network. The equipment of various infrastructures are to be improved, and cross-network information sharing to be realized through isolated exchange technology.

(7) To construct court private cloud

Based on private court network, private mobile network and court extranet, court private cloud is to be built for the high courts and above, to virtualize computing, storage and internet resources. Unified cloud management platforms are to be deployed to form a data center. On-demand service of resources is to be realized, to improve the service ability of various information infrastructure resources.

(8) To construct court open cloud

The high courts (and above) and intermediate courts with actual needs are to rent public cloud by purchasing the service, to form court open clouds. The applications deployed on internet are to be moved to court open cloud under the premise of data security, to improve the internet's application service level and supporting capacity of systems.

(9) To construct secrecy-involving network and secrecy cloud

(Omitted).

(10) To extend the coverage of private court networks

The private court network is to be extended to the courts through wired and wireless communication. Infrastructures supporting the courts' trial information management and audio/video applications are to be deployed, to realize the overall coverage to "the last kilometer".

(11) To upgrade the function and performance of private court networks

The bandwidth capacity is to be expanded. The core network equipment is to realize dual-facility redundancy backup and dual-link upstream connection. Private networks with large capacity, high stability and continuous operation are to be built. The high courts and above are to construct network systems with gigabit access and 10 gigabit core. The localization of networks, computing, storage system software and application software are to be promoted.

(12) To construct private mobile court networks

Supporting platforms of mobile applications are to be built to realize the safe access of court mobile officing terminals. And the operation of such businesses as mobile officing, circuit court and dispatched enforcement are to be supported through the safe isolated exchange system.

(13) To improve the access of court extranet

The high courts and above are to construct court extranet and connect with related institutions through various private lines, e-government intranet, e-government extranet and internet, to support the information exchange, information sharing and business collaboration between governmental institutions.

(14) To construct cross-network exchange systems

The high courts and above, and intermediate and grass-roots courts are to construct isolated non-secrecy exchange system. Intermediate and grass-roots courts can also use the isolated non-secrecy exchange system of local high courts. The high courts and above, and intermediate courts with actual needs, are to construct isolated secrecy exchange system.

(15) To strengthen the construction of information management center and enforcement command center

The intermediate courts and above are to construct information management center and enforcement command center, in a unified way or respectively as needed. The information management center should have functions of unified scheduling, multi-level control and concentrated display, to realize information gathering, information control and security strategy deployment. The enforcement command center should have the function of multi-level command, to realize unified command and real-time audio/video transmission and exchange of enforcement.

(16) To construct standardized litigation service hall

All courts are to construct and improve litigation service halls according to the *Guiding Opinions of the Supreme People's Court on the Construction of Court Litigation Service Centers*, set with technical equipment and information systems, and docked with litigation service platforms, to support online and offline one-stop litigation service.

(17) To promote the audio/video convergence and sharing

The high courts and above are to build integrated audio/video management and scheduling platforms, accessible to the intermediate and grass-roots courts, to realize the audio/video net connection between the four levels of courts. All courts are to construct and improve video systems such as video conference, technical courts, remote arraignment, remote litigation reception, enforcement command and security surveillance, and to complete the HD transformation.

(18) To perfect the construction of technical court

The courts are to be technologized as needed on the basis of judicial work actuality, to meet the requirement of "all-trial recording". The audio/video trial records are to be taken in by the information management center of intermediate courts and above for unified scheduling, and the inspection of the audio/video trial records to be part of trial management. All the courts are to be equipped as needed with mobile (portable) technical courts, and the circuit trail cars to be set with technical court equipment.

(20) To set up data backup centers

The Supreme People's Court is to set up two data backup centers in the south and north, and backup important data there in provincial units, to ensure the safety of availability of the data.

(14) To construct standardized computer rooms

The Supreme People's Court is to decide on or formulate standard for the construction of computer rooms in all the courts, which in turn are to complete the renewal, construction or renting of computer rooms according to the standard.

(21) To promote the construction of digital conference system

Digital conference systems are to be constructed in important places such as meeting rooms for judicial committees and grand courtrooms, supporting applications such as remote business, remote video conference and online training.

4.2.2 All-business and whole-process business application platforms are to be built with the focus on one-stop services

Based on various existing application systems and aimed at the connection of data interfaces, integration of application interfaces, and the expansion and improvement of business functions, an inside integration platform is to be built, centered on the judges with an integration of various application systems such as trials, enforcement, personnel and judicial management; and an outside service platform is to be built centered on the parties and lawyers with an integration of various application systems such as judicial publicity, litigation service and legal advocacy. The internal integration platform and external service platform are to be connected to form an integrated one-stop service platform.

(22) To reform and perfect judicial open platforms

The three judicial open platforms are to be renewed and perfected according to the judicial openness requirements and construction specifications. The breadth and depth of judicial openness is to be expanded. The mainstream technical means of "microblog" ging, WeChat, mobile phone APPs and website are to be fully used, to realize publishing entity information such as electronic evidences, electronic files and audio/video trial records, to realize the timely and exact publicity of all information that should be publicized, to realize the automatic inner-platform and cross-platform association of procedures, documents, enforcement and other related information in the first instance, second instance and retrial, and to realize one-stop information query for the case and co-related cases. Functions such as user navigation, behavior analysis and suggestion collection are to be perfected, and the effect of judicial publicity to be assessed in real time.

(23) To construct platforms for whole-process litigation service

The high courts and above are to construct and improve litigation service networks for the jurisdictional courts, integrate the platforms and functions of online litigation, lawyer service, appeal and letter-petition and people's assessor management, and provide all-process litigation services for the people together with the litigation service halls. The transformation of litigation service from information offer to business participation and from limited procedure participation to whole-process participation is to be supported. Online and offline judicial resources are to be fused for the implementation of online registration, payment, evidence exchange, legal procedure application, file examination, court session, delivery service and mediation. Functions for the collection of user evaluations and problem feedbacks are to be realized. Active participation in the "Internet +" convenience project will be taken, to realize the public service coordination with other related departments.

(24) To set up nationally unified 12368 litigation service hotline

Based on the existing 12368 litigation service hotline in the Supreme People's Court and high courts, the 12368 hotline is to be generalized to cover all the courts. The system of human agent service is to be improved in provincial units, and the nationally unified management and interaction of 12368 message service is to be realized. The functions for the collection of user evaluations and problem feedbacks are to be realized. The service system is to be connected with other litigation service systems and court inner application system of trial enforcement, and to be fully incorporated into the all-process litigation service platforms.

(25) To integrate nationwide court affairs websites

The court affairs websites are to be integrated in provincial units according to the requirements of government affairs website management. Nation language support is to be provided as needed. And the court affairs website groups will be formed based on Chinese Court Net. The column construction such as hot case reports, messages for grand justices, message boxes for the deans, supervision and report, and communication and connection, is to be strengthened. Judicial advocacy is to be carried out simultaneously on new media such as "microblog" ginggings, WeChat, APP clients and mobile TVs.

(26) To upgrade and expand the trial business system, with the focus on the support of lateral integration and vertical coordination.

Based on the *Opinions of the Supreme People's Court about the Comprehensive*

Deepening of Court Reform and related court standard specifications, the trial business system is to be upgraded and expanded in provincial units, with the stress on the integration fusion with other applications such as enforcement and letter-petition, to realize the automatic association of case information. The management of evidences and entity information such as evidence adoption and audio/video trial records is to be realized, electronic litigation archives to be formed, to realize the electronic transfer of appellate files and the automatic generation of judicial statistics. The minority languages are to be supported as needed. The judicial reform requirements, such as cross-regional and multi-case trials, evidence-based judgements, the quick handling of minor criminal cases, case acceptance system, trial judge and collegial panel mechanism, chief judges' supervision mechanism and judicial coordination, are to be supported. And the business coordination between the higher and lower courts, between the courts of different jurisdictions, and between the courts and related governmental institutions (such as procuratorates and prisons) is to be realized.

(27) To enforce the enforcement system with an emphasis on joint enforcement

The Supreme People's Court is to construct node procedure management system for national executive cases. The management and control of node procedures in nationwide executive cases are to be realized, supporting the publicity of the procedures and files of the executive cases. enforcement command systems are to be constructed in high court units, to form an integrated and coordinative operation system among the jurisdiction courts. Internet supervision systems are to be constructed, and the business coordination with the supervised institutions is to be realized as needed. The credit punishment system is to be constructed and perfected, to realize the overall coordination with social credit systems and to form a new mode of credit punishment. The technical support, self-constructed or rented, is to be provided for internet judicial auctions. Property-related enforcement management system is to be constructed to support the unified management of property-related enforcement.

(28) To improve the letter-petition system, aimed at the interconnection of letter-petition business among the four levels of courts

The letter-petition system is to be improved. The interconnection of letter-petition business among the four levels of courts is to be supported. The closure of letter-petitions and the supervision of letter-petition receptions are to be supported. The fusion with litigation service platforms and system connection with letter-petition institutions are to be realized.

(29) To perfect the trial management system while improving precise management capability

Six kinds of judicial management applications (the assessment of case effect, the examination of case quality, the management of trial processes, the analysis on trial situation, the evaluation of trial performance and the management of judicial committee affairs) are to be built and perfected. The automatic assessment of case effect and automatic examination of court-hearings and files are to be realized. The control of node procedures in trials are to be strengthened, to improve trial quality and efficiency.

(30) To construct judicial supporting systems based on smart big data service

The judicial supporting applications of case reference, verdict specification, clue searching and public opinion analysis are to be constructed and perfected, and seamlessly integrated into the judicial business system, to assist the judges' trial work intelligently. The judicial reform requirements, such as unified law application, evidence-based verdict and reasoning judicial files, are to be supported.

(31) To construct the intranets of the four-level courts based on the private court network

The courts are to construct or improve intranets based on the private court network, and the Supreme People's Court is to build the private network portal. Internal web information of the courts is to be integrated, to realize the fusion of information such as instant messages, notifications, posts, information submissions, business exchanges, desktop videos, libraries and professional resources, and to support the information sharing of vertically connected private court networks. The platforms for judge training are to be built, to realize the functions of online judge training and study.

(32) To promote the extension of officing and trial systems to mobile applications

The officing and trial systems are to be promoted in provincial units to extend to mobile applications. Mobile trial handling, officing, meeting, and other functions such as on-site trial recording, file formulation, remote electronic signature and dispatched enforcement (delivery) are to be realized. And the application systems are to be promoted to extend to other judicial business fields.

(33) To construct secrecy-involving application system

(Omitted).

(34) To extend the personnel management system, focusing on associating judges with their cases and performance persons with cases and things

The Supreme People's Court is to perfect the national court personnel management system and construct applications of grading tests of law enforcement qualifications for nationwide court judicial police. All courts are to construct new court personnel management systems to support the judicial reform requirements for personnel classification management, judge position management, judge election management, judge performance management, judge training management and judge salary management, and to integrate it with application systems such as trial enforcement and judicial management to realize the information sharing of personnel, case, administrative affairs.

(35) To expand the judicial management system, and aim at the precise management of judicial affairs

The application systems for judicial management businesses, supporting the management of administrative affairs, archives, discipline inspection, finance, logistics equipment, informatization and judicial auxiliaries, are to be constructed and integrated with the application systems such as trial execution and personnel management, to realize the precise judicial administration management in the light of case, person and event, and to meet the judicial reform demands for the unified management of personnel, finance and properties at sub-provincial levels. The building of information platforms for the concentrated management of local case-involving properties is to be promoted in coordination with related institutions.

4.2.3 A smart service system of information resources is to be constructed to enhance "data management" capability

The high courts and above are to construct trial information database, constantly extend the coverage of data collection, and promote the in-depth integration of various resources. The platforms of big data management and service are to be constructed, the concentrated management, sharing and exchange of the data resources to be strengthened, and the level of intelligent big data service to be enhanced.

(36) To construct trial information database and aim at an overall data coverage

The Supreme People's Court is to construct and perfect the national judicial information database, and high courts are to construct and perfect the jurisdictional judicial information database. According to the standards of court informatization, the range of data resources is to be extended to judicial personnel, judicial affairs, judicial research and informatized management, and to be supplemented external data as needed to form national basical information database. The trial, person, property and external data in the high courts are to be integrated through data association.

(37) To perfect the big data management system, centered on the improvement of data quality

The high courts and above are to construct and perfect big data management systems based on the platforms of big data management and service, supporting distributed data processing, to realize the storage and management of structured, semi-structured, and unstructured data. The application systems of such businesses as trial and enforcement are also supported. All courts are to carry out the catalog management of metadata and information resources. The management of data quality is to be strengthened to ensure data accuracy. A long-term mechanism of mutual data trust is to be built.

(38) To construct data sharing and exchange systems based on the big data management and service platforms

The high courts and above are to construct data sharing and exchange systems based on the big data management and service platforms, to realize the data sharing and exchange inside and between the courts. The interior business coordination and the coordination between the courts and external application systems are both supported.

(39) To construct big data analysis system

The high courts and above are to expand the construction of big data analysis system based on the big data management and service platform. The model of data analysis on trial business, judicial documents and machine learning algorithm is to be constructed. The data in the judicial information database are to be mined, analyzed and displayed by Business Intelligence, big data analysis and visualized means, supporting intelligent big data analyses such as multi-dimensional analysis, correlation analysis and trend prediction.

(40) To develop smart services of judicial openness and litigation service

The high courts and above are to develop intelligent services of judicial publicity and litigation service facing the people and other administrative departments. The publicity and litigation services of litigation service effect analysis, party credit, case winning/losing factor analysis, legislative suggestions, judicial suggestions, social management monograph, case studies, petition consulting and white papers of court trial work are to be offered. The service of outward big judicial data analysis is also offered. These services are to be integrated seamlessly with the application systems of judicial openness and litigation service, to provide more valuable judicial services for the people and other governmental departments.

(41) To develop smart services of decision supporting, monitoring and early warning

The high courts and above are to develop intelligent services of decision supporting, monitoring and early warning, such as intelligent assistance of case handling, intelligent trial decision making, intelligent execution decision making, and the automatic risk recognition and early-warning. These services are to be integrated seamlessly with the application systems of trial execution business and judicial management.

(42) To develop intelligent services for judicial research and performance assessment

The high courts and above, facing judicial management, are to develop smart services for judicial research and performance assessment, such as trial resource configuration assessment, judicial research and guidance, judicial statistical analysis, talent selection and evaluation, intelligent workload evaluation, informatization efficacy evaluation and intelligent video analysis. These services are to be integrated seamlessly with the application systems of managerial decision-making and personnel work, to provide policy-making service for the participation in social management and promotion of socioeconomic development.

4.3 The guarantee systems are to be strengthened in line with the system construction and application demands

Standardized safety guarantee systems, quality and efficient operation guarantee systems and professional talent guarantee systems are to be constructed according to the requirements of court informatization transformation and upgrading, to provide a vigorous support for the sustainable development of informatization construction.

(43) To continue the grading protection of important non-secrecy information

All the courts are to carry out grading and grade recording work at the same time as the construction of informatization systems, according to the *Guiding Opinions on the Grading Work of Grading Important Non-secrecy Court Information Protection*. The information security systems meeting the requirements of the protection grades are to be constructed, and the corresponding safety management systems are to be formulated and implemented, according to the *Basic Requirements of Grading Safety Protection of Court Information System*. The platforms of safety appraisement management are to be built. At least one grade assessment is to be carried out in the operation of the information systems in grade 3 protection. Any inconformity with the standard requirements of the protection grades is to be rectified timely.

(44) To complete the construction and grading protection of secrecy-involving systems

(Omitted).

(45) To build the unified identity authentication system among all court business applications

The Supreme People's Court is to set the technical norms and construction requirements for the unified identity authentication among all court business applications, and to develop the integrating platforms for unified identity authentication. All the courts are to deploy the nodes of the integrating platforms and related equipment, connect with court personnel systems, and integrate with the authentication means of various business applications, to realize the unified user identity authentication among all court business applications.

(46) To build a scientific, quality and efficient operation management system

All the courts are to establish methods for application efficacy evaluation of the information systems, according to the informatization construction and operation management. A quality and efficient operation management system is to be constructed from four aspects of operation organization, operation control, maintenance process and maintenance resources, to optimize the application efficacy of the information systems.

(47) To improve and perfect the operation maintenance systems and mechanisms of infrastructures and applications

The systems of infrastructure operation maintenance are to be improved and perfected, and the monitoring and management of infrastructures in private cloud, open cloud and secrecy cloud environments, such as the monitoring and management of hosts, storage, system software, networks and computer rooms, are to be realized. The systems of application operation maintenance are to be improved and perfected, and the main performance parameters, such as the running state, response time and application load, are to be monitored and managed. Standardized operation maintenance systems and mechanisms of infrastructures and applications are to be constructed and implemented.

(48) To improve and perfect the systems and mechanisms of data maintenance and security maintenance

The operation maintenance management functions of data systems, such as big data management and service platforms and data backup systems, are to be integrated, and data maintenance systems to be constructed, to realize the real-time monitoring and management of such processes as data storage management and data transfer and exchange. Data quality management and data analysis service are to be carried out. Security maintenance systems are to be constructed, and security monitoring and management equipment to be concentrated, to realize safety state monitoring and whole-network safety state analysis. Standardized operation maintenance mechanisms are to be constructed and implemented, to carry out the maintenance of data resources and safety protection systems.

(49) To build emergency response platforms for the information systems

The intermediate Courts and above are to build emergency response platforms as needed for the information systems according to the related emergency response requirements, to realize functions such as emergency on-duty, monitoring and prevention, forecasting and early warning, decision-making assistance, emergency disposal and simulative exercises. Emergency response plans are to be provided, to improve the response ability for different kinds of emergencies.

(50) To construct and generalize visualized operation maintenance platforms

The intermediate courts and above are to build visualized operation maintenance platforms, establish efficacy evaluation index systems for the information systems, integrate the maintenance systems for infrastructures, applications, data and security, evaluate the effect of the information systems based on the information collected by the maintenance systems, and display the evaluations in visualized means.

(51) To fully implement the *Opinions* on talent team construction

The *Opinions on the Construction of Information Talent Teams in the People's Courts* issued by the Supreme People's Court is to be fully implemented. Implementation inspections and assessments are to be carried out regularly. Advanced experiences are to be summarized, problems to be detected, detailed regulations to be formulated and perfected, and the implementation to be supervised and urged, to provide a solid talent guarantee for the rapid development of court informatization construction.

4.4 To enhance application effect through vigorous promotion and effect evaluation

Centering around the fundamental goals of informatization construction, and focused on publicity enhancement and efficacy evaluation, the recognition of court imformatization applications is to be enhanced, the application means of the information system to be ameliorated, and the effect of court imformatization applications to be improved to the full.

(52) To construct a publicity system for the informatization applications

Different publicity resources such as new medias and flat medias are to be integrated. A multi-channel and overall publicity system for the informatization applications is to be constructed. The release announcements, case introduction, efficacy reports and other concerns of the applications are to be publicized, classified and multi-leveled, in service of the public, lawyers, legal workers, and court judges and staff.

(53) To establish a training mechanism for the improvement of application efficacy

The training of judges for the use of trial execution applications and the training of leaders and managerial staff for the use of judicial management applications are to be strengthened, with emphases on the summarization and communication of remarkably effective cases and pilot demonstration projects.

(54) To construct efficacy evaluation systems for judicial service applications

The Supreme People's Court is to construct efficacy evaluation systems for judicial service applications. Satisfaction degrees of the served (such as the masses, lawyers and parties) and feedback suggestions are to be collected, through the functions provided by various judicial service applications, such as satisfaction survey and litigation suggestions. The functions of classified statistics and evaluation are to be provided for administrative staff. And the foundations of sustainable system optimizing are be provided for the application system developers.

(55) To build application efficacy evaluation and improvement mechanisms

Efficacy evaluation mechanisms directed at judicial service applications are to be formed, using the efficacy evaluation systems of the judicial service applications, with the masses, lawyers and parties as main service clients, and the service timeliness and satisfaction degree as focuses. Efficacy evaluation mechanisms directed at the core applications of trial enforcement are to be formed, with judges as service clients, and the application utilization rate, easiness and quickness degree, business supporting ability and intelligent system as focuses. Efficacy evaluation mechanisms directed at judicial management applications are to be formed, with the leaders and managerial staff as service clients, and data application effect, decision supporting ability and the coordinating and integrating ability in management businesses as focuses. The high courts and above are to build among jurisdictional courts mechanisms of evaluation index publishing, index value feedback, index assessment, result publicity, and problem analysis and improvement, to enhance the overall application efficacy of the informatization construction.

5. Guarantee measures

To fulfill the tasks mentioned above and realize the goal of constructing Version 3.0, the courts at all levels are required to be realistic and pragmatic in implementing the following guarantee measures.

5.1 Unifying thoughts and strengthening organization and leadership

The awareness is to be raised that informatization is a guarantee of the strategy of ruling country by law, thus, leaders at all levels and police officers shall regard the construction of people's court modernization as a strategic, fundamental and overall project and synchronize the construction of court informatization with trial and enforcement in terms of deployment, arrangement, implement and inspection; a holistic state management mechanism is to be built to strengthen higher courts' management and supervision of subordinates' court information construction, in which the role of leading groups at all levels in leading and guiding the information construction of courts is to be fully played, thereby securing an effective implementation of tasks.

5.2 Cultivating excellent information talents and enhancing the team strength

Given the fact that the court information construction covers a wide range of aspects and that it has developing difficulties, a talent team of various professions, reasonable hierarchical structure and sufficient quantity of personnel is to be built, which demands cultivating, introducing, selecting and training information and management personnel in practice so that they can play a leading role in court informatization, thereby providing a sound organizational guarantee for court information construction.

5.3 Increasing investment of funds and optimizing resource allocation

The Five-year development plan for information construction of the People's courts at all levels is to be docked with local economy and the 13th five-year plan so as to win governments' support and broaden financial channel, thus increasing investment in the information guarantee system concerning security, operation and maintenance and technical personnel and application efficiency enhancement as well; more efforts are to be put to the work with regard to approval, financial support and implementation of planned projects, so as to ensure local government investment arriving in full and on time; a budget management of information construction is to be strengthened through making a budget in accordance with five-year plan and building a consultation and coordination system of budgeting along with financial departments; the mutual promotion of optimal allocation of information resources and information application is to be realized through preventing redundant construction and a waste of money.

5.4 Intensifying science and technology research and realizing innovation-driven development

It is advised that support for researches in cutting-edge technology and local governments and industry sectors' investment in science and technology should be increased so as to solve problems arising in the modernization of judicial system and judicial capacity; the competitiveness of court information-based industries is to be improved through carrying out strategies of intellectual property and technical standards; the Supreme People's Court and high people's courts are to establish strategic alliance in the field of major information technology, thus forming an operation mechanism of complementary advantages, collaboration, sharing risks and benefits; the planning system of national scientific and technological cooperation is to be perfected through building a center of court information construction and a platform of scientific and technological cooperation, thereby realizing innovation-driven development of court informatization.

5.5 Enhancing the strict management of construction with systematic methods

It's recommended that court informatization dock with the deployment of T*he Thirteenth Five-year Plan for National Economic and Social Development*, and keep in tune with such special plans as *The Thirteenth Five-year Plan for National Government Information Construction* and local economic and social development; more efforts should be put to strengthen their role in guiding the implementation of annual plan and arrangement of major projects so as to ensure the implementation of construction; an interlocking implementation system of informatization planning with a single objective be built through strengthening connection between superior courts and subordinates; the courts at all levels should submit an annual report of informatization and development plan; the whole process management of information construction should be strengthened to reinforce project supervision, with construction procedures being standardized, and a strict system of budget adjustment and file management being carried out.

5.6 Strengthening anti-corruption consciousness and constructing the information system in accordance with law and regulations

In face of the large investment and high integrity risk of information construction, the courts at all levels are advised to strengthen probity education among technical and administrative personnel so as to train them to practice "Three Stricts and Three Steadies" consciously, raise their awareness of law and discipline and be subjected to internal and external supervision through building an integrity risk preventing and controlling mechanism; unremitting efforts are to be put to the construction of a clean government: insisting collective discussion on major projects, building a scientific and standard system of project management, supervising and auditing concerning such links as project approval, purchase, invitation for bids, review, acceptance check and fund utilizing, making decisions about major fund utilizing and major issues in information construction according to regulations; discipline inspection and supervision institutions are to intensify administration and system surveillance, thereby creating a clean and positive environment for information construction.

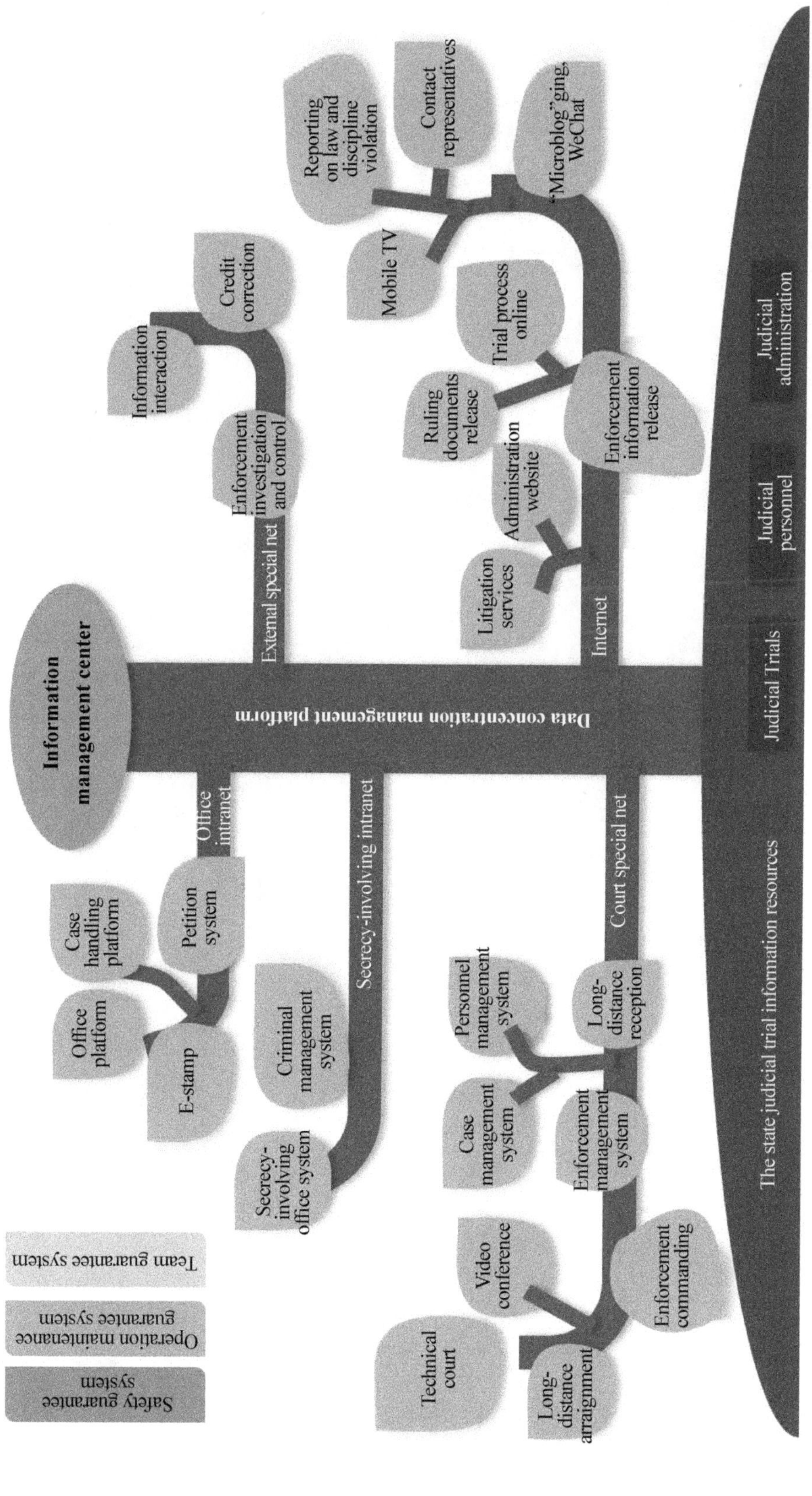

Fig. 1 An ever green tree of informatization of the people's court Version 2

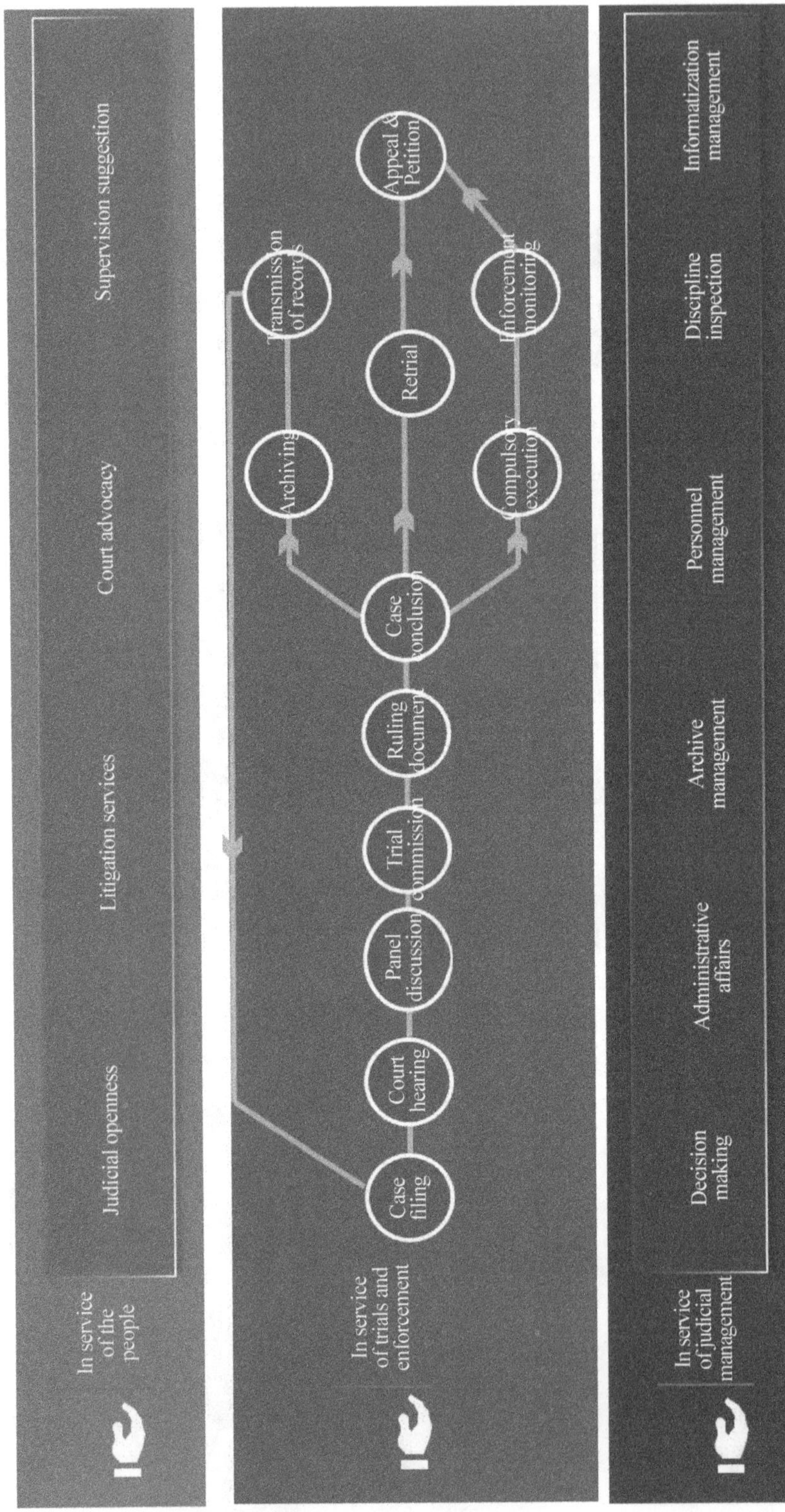

Fig. 2 Framework of the people's court business

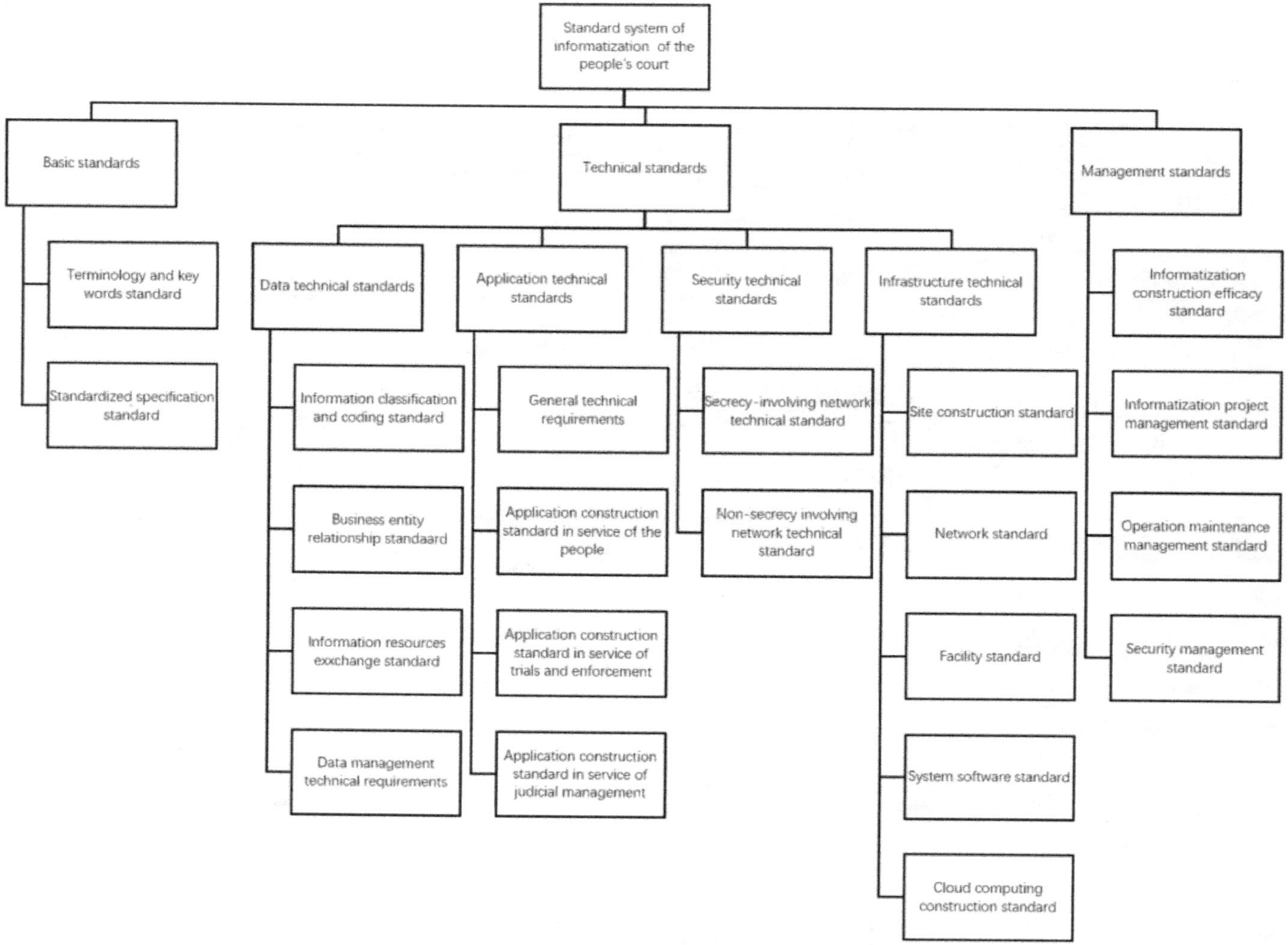

Fig. 3 Target of informatization of the people's court – Informatization standardization construction

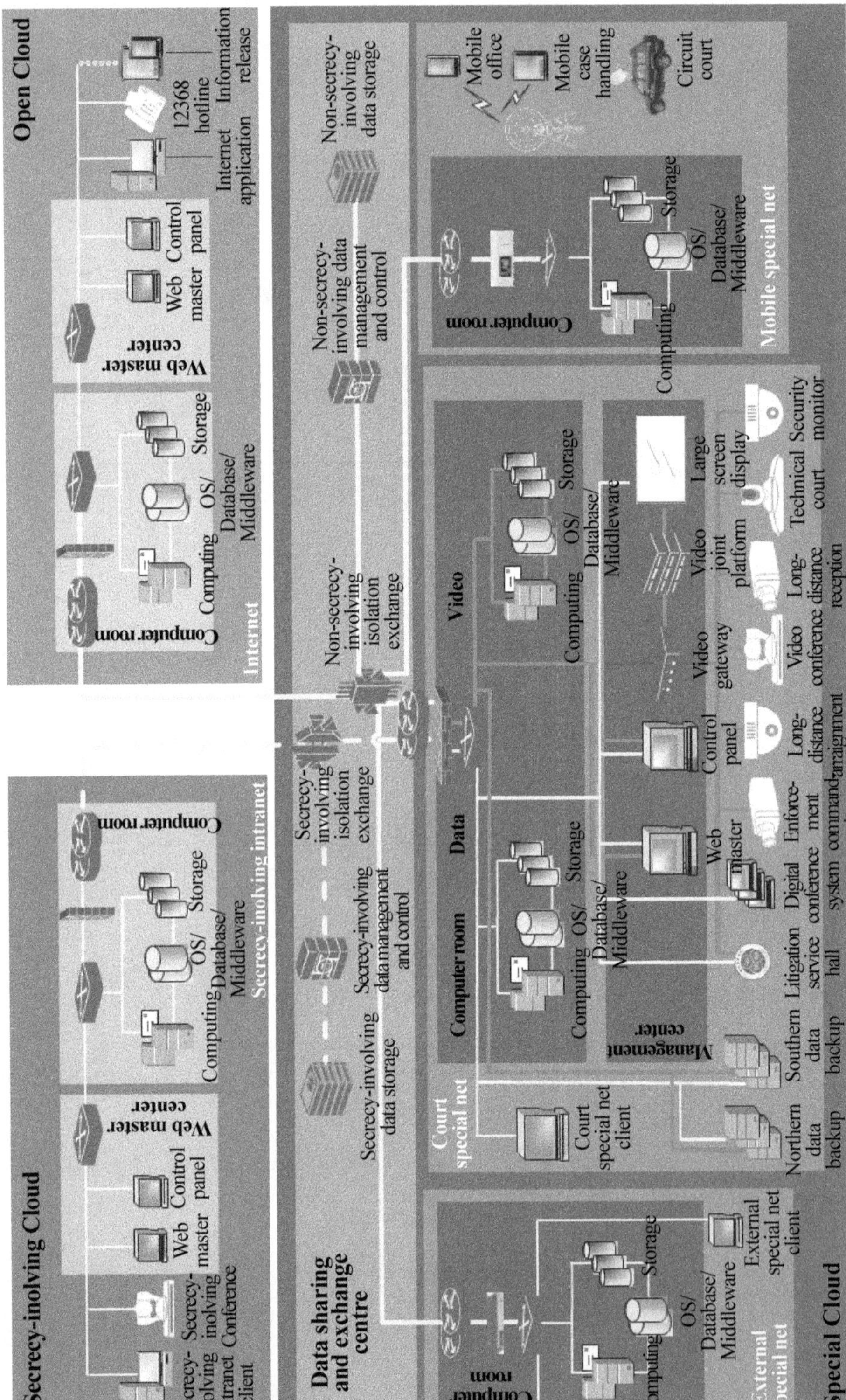

Fig. 4 Target of informatization – Infrastructure construction

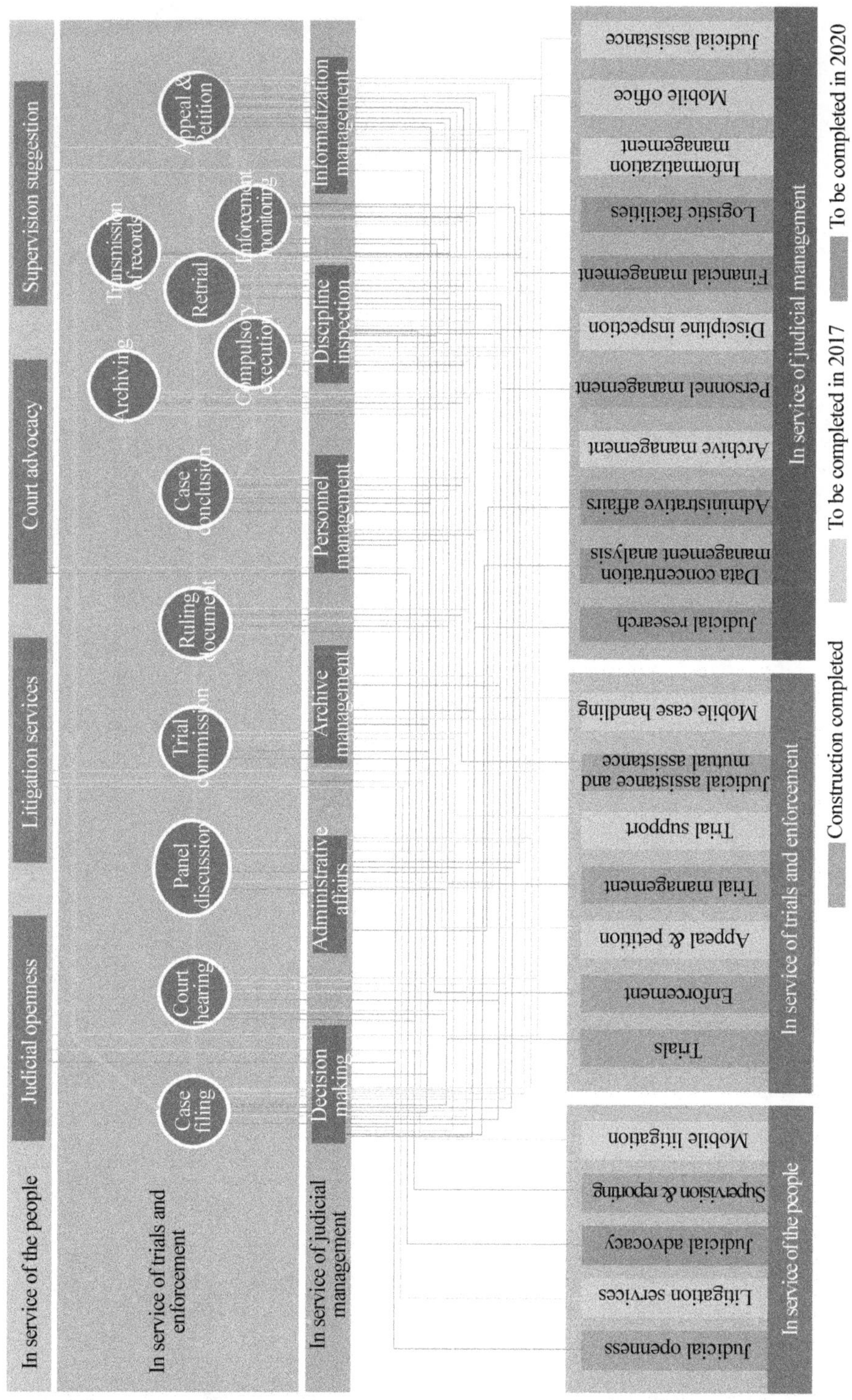

Fig. 5 Target of informatization – Application construction

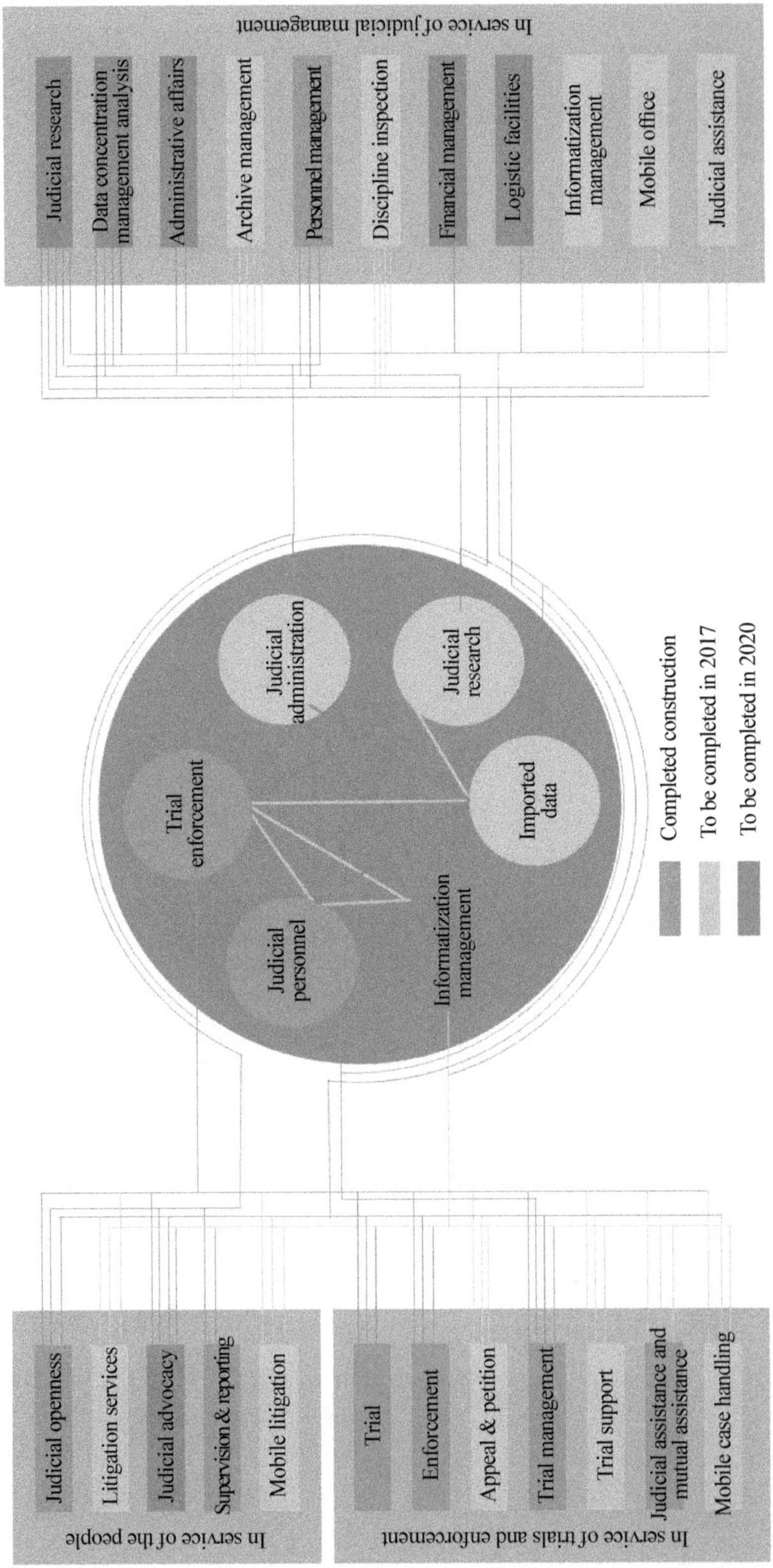

Fig. 6 Target of informatization – Information resources construction

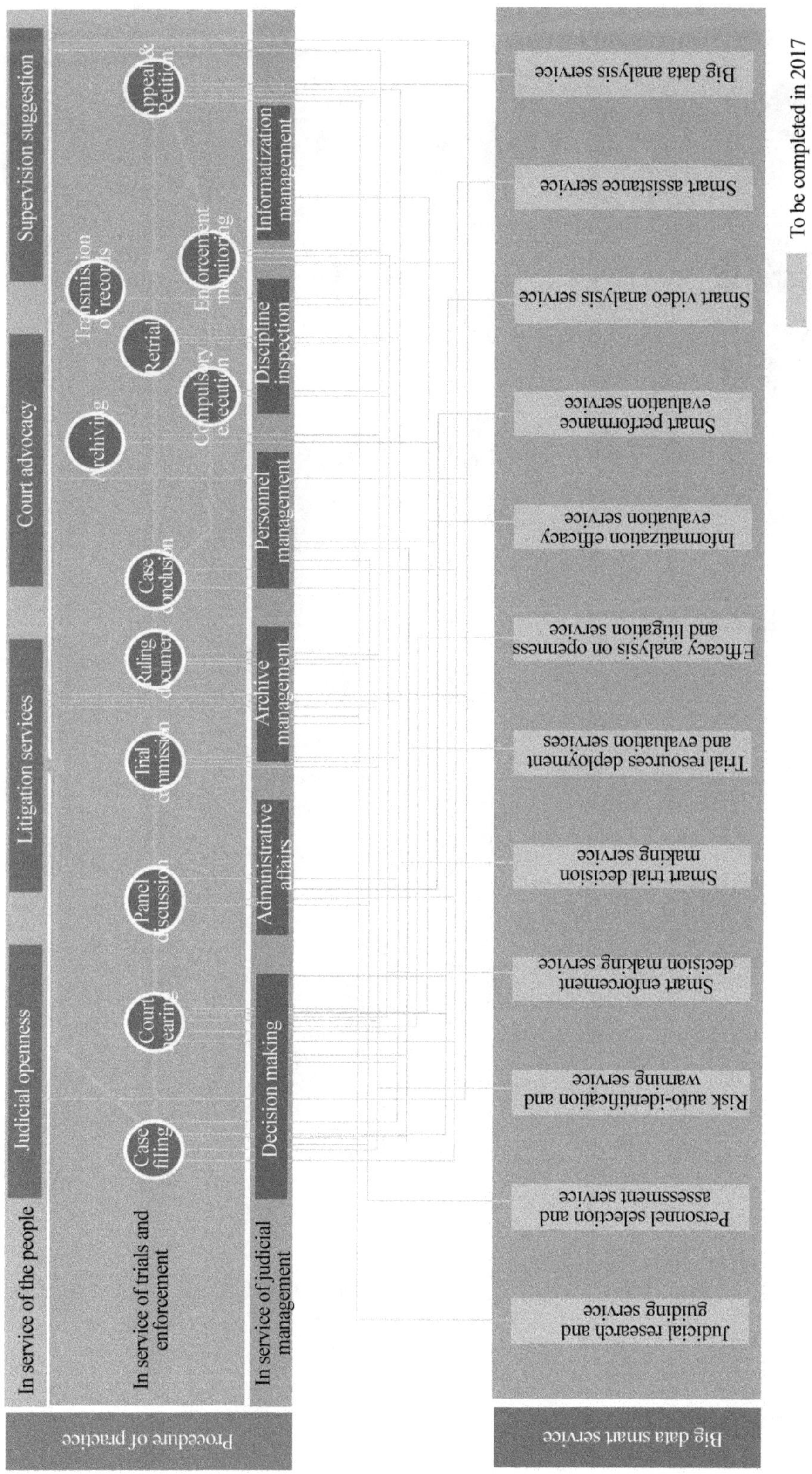

Fig. 7 Target of informatization of courts – Big data services

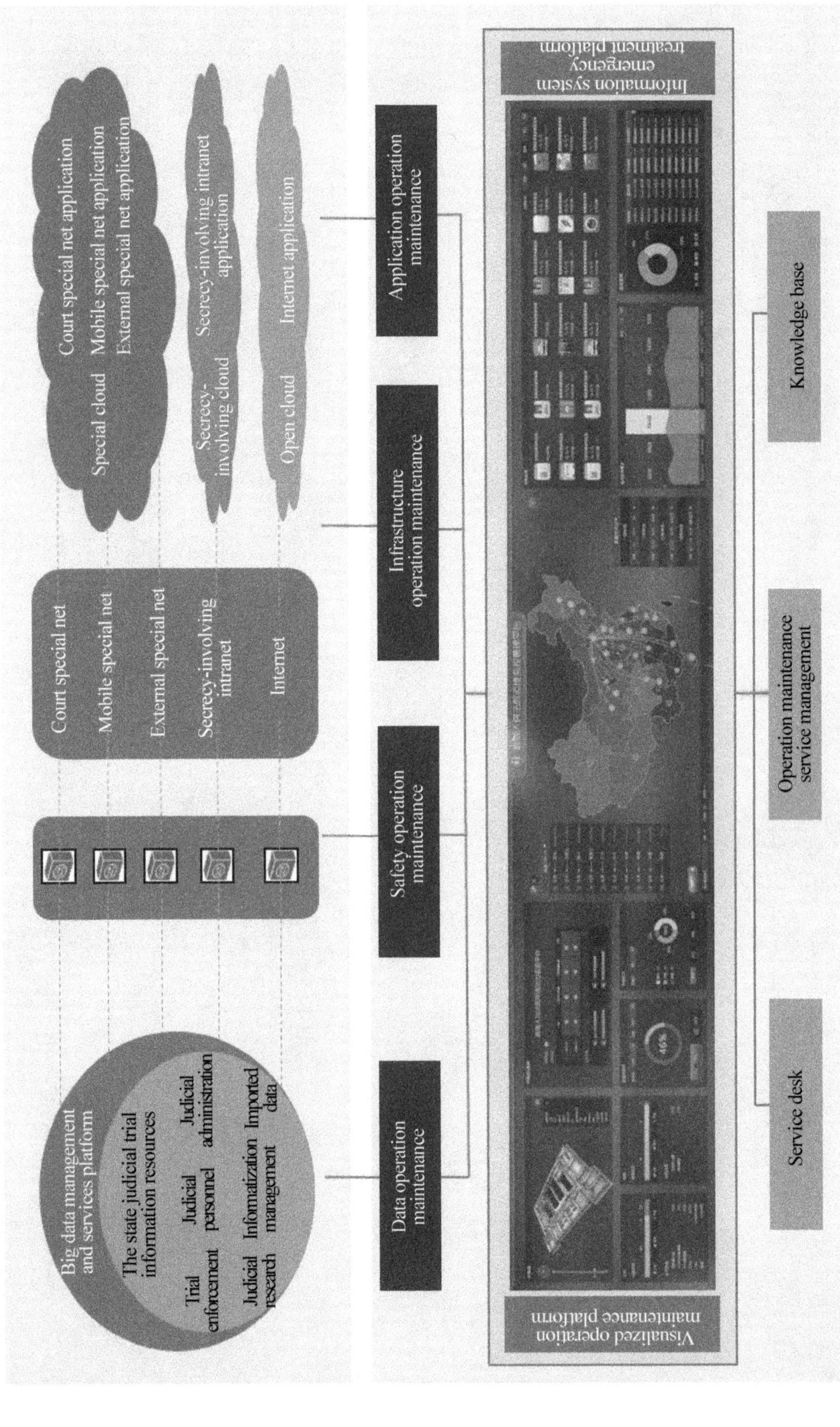

Fig. 8 Target of informatization – operation maintenance guarantee system

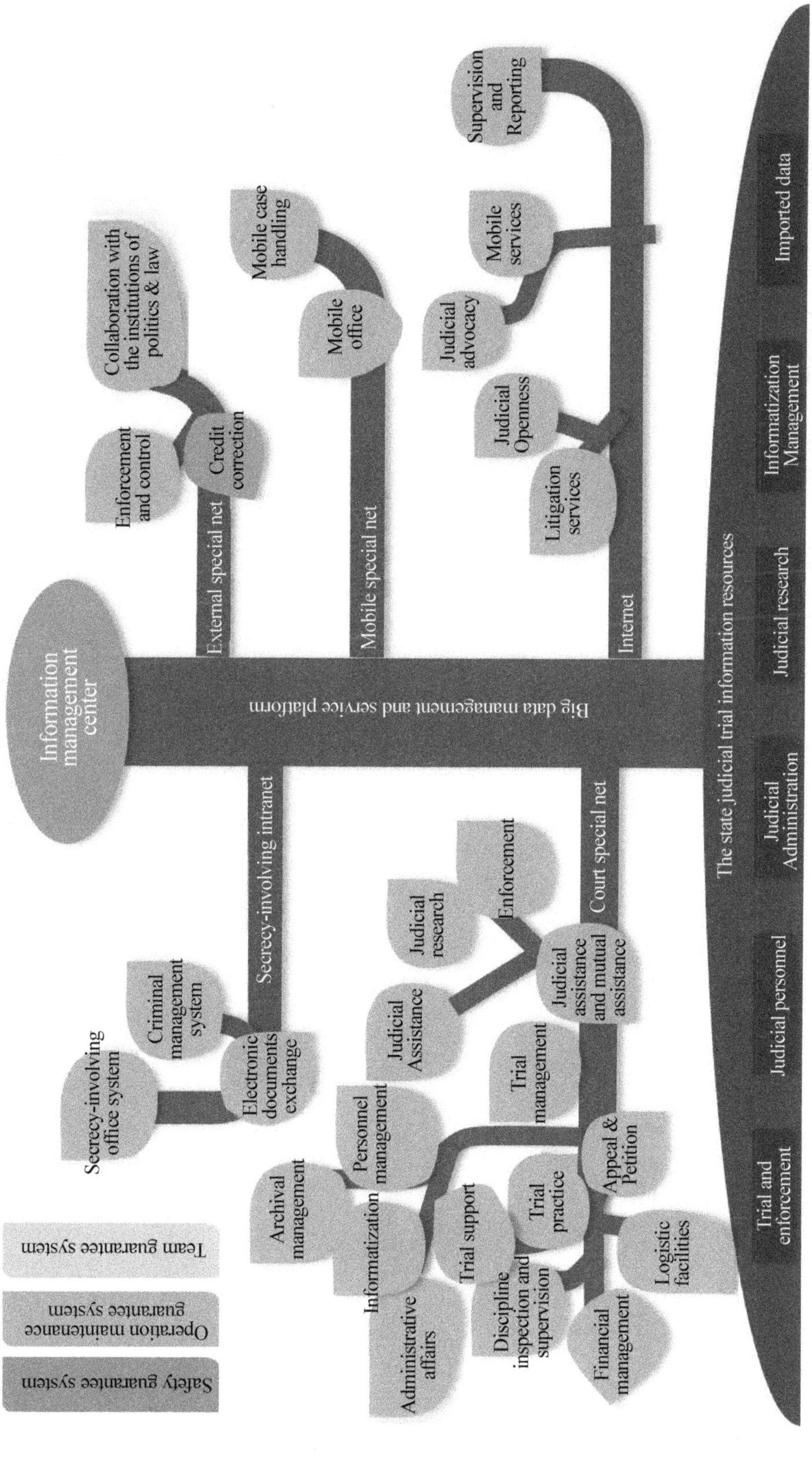

Fig. 9 An ever green tree of informatization of the people's courts Version 3.0

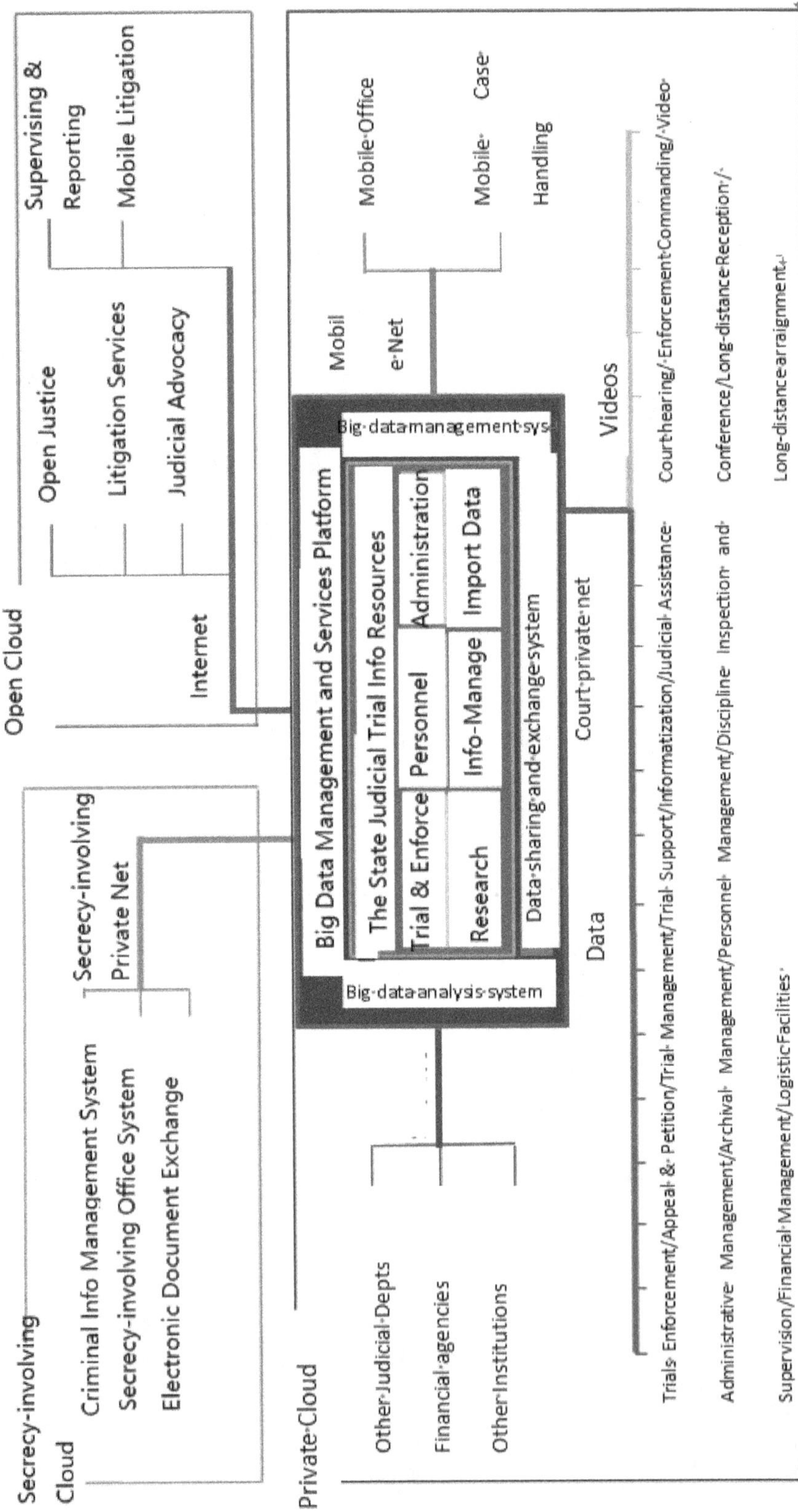

Fig. 10 A general framework of the informatization of the people's courts

This book is the result of a co-publication agreement between China Social Sciences Press (China) and Paths International Ltd (UK)

Title: A Third Party Evaluation Report on the Informatization of Chinese Courts
Editor in Chief: Tian He
Executive Editor: Lv Yanbin
ISBN: 978-1-84464-555-8
Ebook ISBN: 978-1-84464-556-5

Paths International Ltd
www.pathsinternational.com
Published in the United Kingdom

CPSIA information can be obtained
at www.ICGtesting.com
Printed in the USA
LVHW062116271020
670009LV00004B/15

9 781844 645558